A FOURTH
KENTISH
PATCHWORK

First published 1974
© *Robert H. Goodsall 1974*

TEXT SET IN BASKERVILLE TYPE AND
PRINTED IN ENGLAND BY HEADLEY BROTHERS LIMITED
109 KINGSWAY LONDON WC2B 6PX AND ASHFORD KENT

BELL HARRY TOWER, CANTERBURY

ROBERT H. GOODSALL

A Fourth
Kentish Patchwork

STEDEHILL PUBLICATIONS
HARRIETSHAM
KENT

CONTENTS

LIST OF ILLUSTRATIONS

LIST OF ILLUSTRATIONS

Between pages 72 and 73

William Wriothesley Turner Baldwin
Mrs. Dorothy L. Ascherson when living at Stede Hill
Harrietsham school fete held on the Booth Field, 14th July, 1971

Between pages 76 and 77

Practising Country Dances in the Nineteen-Twenties
Cricket on the Booth Field
Brisk business at a Church Fete

Between pages 80 and 81

Shakespeare Cliff
Margate about 1831
St. Lawrence High Street
The Thanet Shore

Between pages 96 and 97

William Somerset Maugham as a boy at King's
Portrait painted by Sir Gerald Kelly, R.A.
Whitstable Vicarage shortly before its demolition in 1973
All Saints' Church in the time of the Rev. Maugham
The Norman Staircase
The Dark Entry
The way to the King's School from Canterbury West Railway
    Station
Whitstable, after the drawing by J. M. W. Turner
Seasalter, The Battery, to-day

Between pages 104 and 105

Robert Smuthe Hichens, about 1914
The Rev. Arthur John Galpin, M.A.
'Meadowside', Tankerton-on-Sea, Kent
The author in his 6 h.p. Rover car
Mrs. George Holden
Dr. Charles E. Etheridge
The Cross, Whitstable, about 1900
The author's wife having her fortune told at Biskra
Taormina below the snow-capped summit of Etna

FOREWORD

ONCE AGAIN when completing the writing of a book—in this case the fourth of the Patchwork series—it becomes my pleasure and duty to acknowledge the valuable help I have received from many quarters. Some is already mentioned in the text but more remains to be specially noted here.

My friend, R. H. Hiscock, LL.B., F.S.A., Chairman of Council, Kent Archaeological Society, most kindly read through the proofs of "Water-Borne Trade on the Medway", corrected some mistakes and suggested several additions of fact for which I am most grateful. The late Arthur R. Cook was equally helpful in providing first-hand information concerning the development and trade of cement-making.

I am much indebted to Mrs. J. Haynes of Wye, for allowing me to make a copy of the manuscript notes on Wateringbury of the bell-ringer, Richard James Newman, whilst a great deal of assistance in the compilation of the Harrietsham School story came not only from the much respected Maidstone Notary Public, Mr. P. G. M. Monckton, who overlooked the script with a lawyer's eye, but also from the Reverend Doctor S. G. Brade-Birks, M.SC., D.SC., F.S.A., of Godmersham, Mrs. D. L. Ascherson, Mrs. Sylvia Willard, and Mr. S. A. Pope.

My special thanks are due to Mrs. Mary West for making the charming little pen-drawing identified by her signature used as tail-pieces.

Mr. C. J. Wright, previously unknown to me, has taken much trouble to elucidate the mysterious identity of the "Observant Pedestrian" who figures in the account of Samphire. I deeply appreciate his kindness.

In compiling the account of the association of Somerset Maugham and Robert Hichens with Whitstable and Canterbury, I have received most valuable assistance from Paul Pollak, M.A., O.K.S., and Housemaster of the King's School's Marlowe House, who not only read the proof, made suggestions for the inclusion of additional facts, and acted as intermediary in respect of portrait illustrations which had previously appeared in the *Cantuarian*. Also he put me in touch with Mr. Anthony Curtis, Literary Editor of the *Financial Times*, the author of a recently published book on Somerset Maugham commemorating the centenary of that famous author's birth. For the great trouble Mr. Pollak has taken, I am much in his debt. I am also glad of the opportunity to acknowledge the permission I received from he late Sir Compton Mackenzie to quote from his *My Life and Times*, also from Messrs. A. P. Watt and Sons, the Literary Executors of W. Somerset Maugham and William Heinerman, who also act in respect of the estate of Robert Hichens, for their general permission to quote extracts from the works of these two authors.

Mr. Douglas West, A.I.B.P., of Whitstable, has been most helpful not only in taking special photographs to illustrate the Maugham and Hichens scene but also by searching through his large collection of photographic records of the town for portraits of two well-known and respected residents of former years who figure in my account. I am most appreciative of this conribution. Similarly I have to thank Mr. W. Lapthorne, Local and Naval Historian, of Broadstairs for allowing me to reproduce three items from his extensive collection of Kent prints.

To all of these I say "Thank you for your interest and help".

1

WATER-BORNE TRADE ON THE MEDWAY

O SERIOUS ATTEMPT was made to render the Medway truly navigable above Maidstone for commercial traffic until Charles II returned to this country and his throne in 1660. No doubt during the middle ages and earlier light water-borne loads were at times transported downstream from the Tonbridge area, but the untamed river must have presented frustrations and hazards to all but quite small boats.

Mention of the Medway appears in very early records—as far back as A.D. 86 flood water was recorded as being the cause of several deaths in the Maidstone region, while in A.D. 666 King Egbert deposited the bodies of his murdered nephews, Ethelred and Ethelbert, in the river. Two hundred years later serious flooding is mentioned whilst in 1114 the opposite conditions prevailed, there was 'a failure of water'.

From the Thames estuary upstream to Maidstone and a little beyond the story is different; from prehistoric and Roman times considerable use of the tidal reaches must have been made for transporting weighty loads. For example, it is reasonable to assume that some at least, if not most, of the pottery produced by the Romans at their Upchurch kilns was taken away by boats, similarly the Kent ragstone quarried in the Maidstone area, both by the Romans and the Normans could most easily reach its destination, particularly to London, by water via the Yantlet (the early name was Yenlade) Creek and the Thames.

This export of stone and other materials, such as fullers earth from the Boxley beds, wool and agricultural produce, could more easily be moved by water than along the generally inferior Kentish roads.

By the end of the 16th century the volume of shipping using the river had grown to such proportions that the Maidstone Corporation was empowered by Charter to levy tolls for wharfage, anchorage and groundage, on all ships coming to the town, also to charge reasonable fees for their loading and unloading.

Up to this time, however, no serious attempt was made to improve the waterway; in many places the banks were badly scoured or broken away while vessels making the passage were at the complete mercy of the tide, the river, in fact, was tidal up to East Farleigh. There were no locks and in periods of heavy rainfall the water level was liable to rise with alarming rapidity, sometimes as much as eighteen feet in forty-eight hours at Teston Bridge, with consequent disasterous flooding lower down.

Nothing was done to rectify these conditions until the reign of Charles II. During his years in exile in the Low Countries the future king became deeply impressed with the skill of the Dutch engineers in draining and improving their countryside and its many waterways. Shortly after his accession to the throne a Bill was presented to Parliament to improve the Medway for navigation. This Bill became an Act in 1664 but for some unexplained reason official interest in the matter ceased and no improvements materialized.

Under the charter of 1559 the Maidstone Corporation was given powers to regulate and control fishing in the Medway between Hawkwood and East Farleigh bridge, but it would seem that the Mayor, Jurats and Commonalty had no grant of the actual fishery as their property although fishing must always have provided a livelihood for those living on or near the river banks.

Between 1625–1628 the Corporation was in dispute with the distinguished local landowner, Sir John Astley* over fishing rights opposite his domain—the Archbishop's Palace and the College buildings. Details of this will be found in *Records of Maidstone*,† published by the Corporation in 1926, but it is not clear if Sir John's estate included a 'several fishery' in that part of the river.

---

* The story of the Astley association with the district is told in my paper 'The Astleys of Maidstone', *Archaeologia Cantiana*, Vol. LXXII, 1958.
† See pages 87, 88, 92, 94 and 237.

Below the county town commercial fishery in the lower reaches of the river must have resulted in considerable use of the waterway by suitable small craft particularly those employed in oyster dredging.

In the reign of George II Parliament passed an Act for regulating, well ordering, governing, and improving the Oyster Fishery in the River *Medway* and Waters thereof, under the authority of the Mayor and Citizens of the City of *Rochester*, in the County of *Kent*.

It had been customary for timber and the products of the Wealden ironmasters in the Lamberhurst, Bayham, Pembury and Horsmonden areas to use the Medway from Twyford or Yalding for transportation but to reach such loading places haulage over the inferior Wealden roads was necessary and this resulted in great damage to the highways particularly in wet seasons. In April 1672, when the parish of Marden applied to the Justices for permission to levy a rate to help in the repair of their roads they advanced the plea that many miles of stone causeways had been 'spoyled of late ... by the much carrying of great guns and timber'.

Efforts to improve the navigation of the river under the Charles II Act having proved more or less abortive, the undertakers, to quote Hasted (Vol. I, p. cxxvii),

procured another in the 13th of king *George* II anno 1740, by which they are incorporated by the name of the proprietors of the navigation of the river Medway, and enabled to raise 30,000l. among themselves to carry on their work; which sum was to be divided into three hundred shares, of which no one person was to have more than ten. They were empowered likewise to employ boats, &c. to carry goods on the river, and to take toll of others; and the navigation was exempted from the commission of sewers; in consequence of which, the proprietors have laid out great sums of money in deepening, and widening it, and erecting locks and bridges, and other improvements; insomuch, that a safe and constant navigation upon it is now completed, from Rochester up to Tonbridge; by which the great quantities of fine timber, which grown in the wealds of Kent and Sussex, and the iron ordnance, balls, and other materials of war forged in those parts, which could not otherwise, by reason of the badness of the roads, be conveyed to market, without an enormous expence, find an easy carriage in

3

lighters thither; and wood, corn, grain, hay, hops, wool, leather, and all manner of provisions, coals, lime, quarrystone, and all other necessaries and commodities, are conveyed on it at an easy expence, to the great benefit of this country, and the improvement of trade and commerse in general.

The *traffic* on the Medway still increases (i.e. in 1778) from the neighbouring country on each side of it, till it comes to Maidstone, where it becomes still more considerable by the hoys, which continually sail from thence freighted for the supply of the London markets; to which the several mills for corn, paper, &c. there, and the great quantity of hop-ground in those parts, do not a little contribute . . .

At Rochester-bridge, where the tide of this river becomes exceeding rapid, foaming with great noise as it passes through, all the shipping is obliged to stop, neither the bridge, nor the river itself, permitting them to sail higher; and at those towns of Strood, Rochester and Chatham, they unload their cargoes, either for sale there, or to be put into lighters to be conveyed upwards, towards Maidstone, or Tunbridge.

Through the centuries Rochester Bridge has always represented a formidable obstacle to upriver traffic, particularly the medieval structure which was replaced in 1856 by the one erected for the Bridge Wardens by William Cubitt; the narrow arches, massive piers and cut-waters of the earlier bridge made the passage by such small craft as could get through something of a hazard and the situation was not improved when the adjacent rail bridge was erected to carry the London, Chatham and Dover lines. Inevitably these barriers effectively prevented any large sea-going vessels from proceeding up-river from Rochester. The 1856 road bridge and the 1858 London, Chatham & Dover Railway bridge each had a 'swing' section to allow river traffic to pass easily, but when the rail bridge was renewed in 1892 both in this and the road bridge the 'swing' sections were eliminated.

However, by the skill of crews, small craft could always 'shoot the bridge' on the flood tide provided the recognized 'drill' was followed so that lighters and barges regularly traded to Maidstone or beyond. Spritsail barges were provided with the necessary gear to enable the crew to lower the mast sail and cordage onto the deck when passing under bridges. Edgar J.

[View of the City of Rochester.]

₊ The Office of the Society for the Diffusion of Useful Knowledge is at 59, Lincoln's Inn Fields.
LONDON:—CHARLES KNIGHT, 22, LUDGATE STREET, AND 13, PALL-MALL EAST.
Printed by WILLIAM CLOWES, Duke Street, Lambeth.

March, in his *Spritsail Barges of Thames and Medway*, gave an interesting account on how the operation was carried out.*

The gear of these Medway barges works very easily, being in frequent use. It is most interesting to watch a barge shooting Rochester bridge with the flood tide under her. It is customary to engage the services of a third hand—the huffler—to assist in this operation. Sculling out on his tubby little boat, he boards the upward-bound swimmie and lets his skiff trail behind. The fact that two boats are in tow is a sure sign that a Huffler is on board. He then goes for'ard and stands over the huff—the square part of the overhanging swim from which his particular name is derived. The barge rounds the bend and stands on until it seems the topmast must collide with the first bridge, then the stayfall is eased away, and the great weight of spars, mast and sails, is lowered back on to the main hatch covers, a jumble of picturesque confusion, which it

* Percival Marshall, 1948, p. 43.

5

seems an impossible task ever to disentangle. Carrying her way, the barge drives on under the railway bridge through which the current sets diagonally, and as soon as she is clear of the road bridge the huffler and mate are at the windlass. The pawls click merrily as the men turn with all their might, slowly heaving up the gear—all five tons in weight—just as it is with all sail set, and in a matter of moments the barge is on her way up river, every stitch is drawing and the services of the huffler are no longer needed.

If the wind be light, steerage way can only be kept on the barge by some hard pulling on the heavy sweeps; nearer the arch the tide gets a greater hold and hurries her through.

Throughout the 19th-century and up to the outbreak of the Second World War the spritsail barge was the craft almost exclusively employed in the carrying trade on the Medway above Rochester. These remarkable vessels of shallow draught and fine sailing qualities were designed to be crewed by only two men, the skipper and his mate and have never been surpassed in fitness for the work they were called on to do. It is sad that mechanical power rather than the winds of heaven has brought to an end the commercial use of these lovely vessels.

During the reign of Elizabeth I, Maidstone had four wharfs or landing-places on the Waterside, while five hoys or sea-going vessels, ranging from 30 to 50 tons burden were registered locally. By 1839, according to *The Topography of Maidstone and its Environs*, eleven firms were operating barge sailings from the town mostly to wharfs in the Pool of London on a twice weekly schedule, one however offered to carry goods 'to all parts'. The names of these owners were:

Simmons & Sons	Sailings to	Kent Wharf
Mason	do.	Liddiard's Wharf
Barlow, Gill & Hills	do.	Hays and Kent and Sussex Wharfs
Dedrick	do.	Bensted's Wharf
Chaplin		
Wimble		
Poolley		Destination not stated.
Pybus		
Selmes & Jackson		

From early times an important quay a little below the town was New Hythe which served much local commerce, particularly the export of ragstone.

A peak in the river traffic may well have been reached in 1906 when the small steamer 'Pioneer' arrived at one of the town wharves with a cargo of coal from Goole.*

For two centuries or more the seaborne trade between the town and the north of England was considerable; a late eighteenth-century letter preserved at the Maidstone Museum confirms this.

To Messrs Brenchley Stacey & May   Rochester
Byeports   Maidstone   Octo^r 11th 1788.
       For Geo May
Dr Friend

I received thy favors ordering 4 Grose of Bottles—that Order I sent to the North by Captⁿ Stevenson, Mas(ter) of my ship Friendship—he has lately been here & is now in ballast—the very great demand prevented his haveing them when last there, he is to bring them up on his return; my Friend may depent on their comeing, it shall not slip my memory.

Please to tell Mr Stacey we dare not attempt to bringing stones in blowing weather, its to hazardous. We have loaded a barge for you with 37 Cha(ldrons) of Tanfield coals— I wish for one more barge immediately for you, it may be a long while before we get back with an other cargo & and you may be out.

The Tanfield ship has been several days in this river, gales of wind & bad tydes hinder^d; she carried away her Bowsprit, Cathead & c^r against the Grampos, man of war at Chatham.

         I am with kind respects
             Your oblige^d Fr^d
                Thos White.

P.S.

The Barge went thro Bridge this morning tyde. Should think she must be nearly up at Maidstone. Pray send an other off or the ship will be detained or you out before she comes again.

It would be interesting to know the nature of the contents of the '4 Grose of Bottles' ordered by Mr. George May. Could it have been 'Scotch'?

The 1739 Act of Parliament for making the river navigable

* Maidstone Civic Archives.

above Maidstone had an immediate and profound effect on the industrial fortunes of the then small town of Tonbridge and commerce throughout the whole area. The Company of Proprietors of the Navigation of the River Medway, to quote the full title, was formed to implement the provisions of the Act. Money was subscribed by a number of prominent people in the county in the form of £100 shares which resulted in a working capital of some £14,000 and the task of canalizing the waterway, building locks and establishing towpaths was started; by October 1741 the river was opened for traffic.

The Company bought its own barges and two years later commenced to trade as coal merchants and dealers in timber, stone, iron, lime and other bulky products. At first the return to investors was meagre but during the best years of the Company's trading there was a rise in the value of the stock to £450 per share. But in 1892 with the last payment of a dividend shareholders received only 2½ per cent.

By 1775 Rochester's medieval bridge of five arches which spanned the river immediately east of the Castle and carried the main highway through the town was becoming decrepit through age and was proving a nuisance to the trading vessels so it was demolished and was replaced by a new structure of three wider arches, much of the old stone being re-used particularly for the parapets; then in 1818 these parapets were replaced by iron railings which completely spoiled the design and former pleasing character.

It was in 1792 that the Lower Medway Navigation Company was incorporated and the important tidal lock at Allington, some two miles below Maidstone was constructed. Previously there had been a ford at the spot, the approximate head of low-tide navigation, where a road led down from the Pilgrims' Way on the North Downs to the river bank by the *Malta Inn*. From here on down to the Thames Estuary the tidal waters have always been available for use by such vessels as could negotiate Rochester and Aylesford bridges, the latter having had a wide central span built to replace the narrow medieval arches.

Immediately below Rochester Bridge the Medway, continually widening as it approaches the Estuary, has always been open to sea-going craft for it represents one of the finest deep-water anchorages anywhere round our shores. 'The channel of the river is so deep' Bagshaw wrote in 1847 in his *History of the County of Kent* 'the bed so soft, and the reaches so short, that it is the best and only safe harbour in the kingdom for the larger ships of the royal navy, which ride here when put out of commission in great numbers as in a wet dock, and being moored with chains, which are fixed for that purpose at the bottom of the river, swing up and down with tide'. Shipbuilding and repairs for the Navy at the two great dockyards of Sheerness and Chatham form an important chapter in the river story as do the incursions of the Dutch. However, these are subjects which do not concern us here.

But the mercantile trade of the Medway towns, Strood, Rochester, Chatham and Gillingham, Queenborough and Sheerness is another matter; over the centuries this had grown to great importance, particularly in recent times and will be considered later.

Over the centuries the river has provided a valuable means of exporting various products from the bordering countryside. Ragstone and timber have already been mentioned, while agriculture has always made use of the Medway for carrying loads of wool, grain, hay, hops and various other crops to other parts of the county, to London, or more distant destinations, but additionally there were a number of important products, peculiar to the Maidstone and Rochester areas, that needed water transport for their export. One of these was the fuller's earth found at Boxley and along the tributary Len which was so necessary to the clothweaving craft, a subject I referred to in the third volume of this *Patchwork* series.*

Another natural product which called for water transport was copperas found in the Isle of Sheppey† and shipped to all parts of the country or abroad via the Swale or from Queenborough and Sheerness. Similarly when the papermills came into being, particularly in and around Maidstone, much of the paper was moved to its destination by water, but one of the most important trades developed along the banks of the Medway below the County Town was the burning of lime from the ample

---

* *A Third Kentish Patchwork*, pp. 58–59.
† See my paper *The Whitstable Copperas Industry. Archaeologia Cantiana*, Vol. LXX, 1956.

chalk deposits and later the manufacture of cement, particularly at Snodland.

For many centuries lime has been used as a dressing for agricultural land and lime-burning was carried out in all parts of the country where chalk was available and notably where out-crops occurred along the banks of the Medway and Thames.

Samuel Bagshaw in his 'History' recorded that at Snodland there were 'extensive lime works, established about 1820. The metropolis, which was at one time principally supplied from Dorking in Surrey, now receives an immense quantity from this place'.

From time immemorial burnt chalk, i.e. lime, mixed with sand and wetted, provided mortar for bedding flints, stones or bricks used in wall building, but in 1796 James Parker, a Surrey man developed a product he called 'Roman Cement', using as the raw material the stony nodules called 'clay-stones' found in the cliffs at Swalecliffe, Beltinge, Sheppey and various places on the Essex shore. At Northfleet on the Thames these nodules were burned to produce the 'cement'. Then, twenty years later, a certain Joseph Aspdin evolved a process for producing a greatly improved material destined to revolutionize building technique by mixing brick loam with chalk and burning to convert the mixture into 'Portland' cement. Six years later, in 1830, Major-General C. W. Pasley who was serving at Chatham, brought the process to perfection when, in place of brick loam, he substituted the blue clay of the Medway. Details of the subsequent story of cement manufacture were given to me in 1970 by my friend Arthur Cook, now unhappily no longer with us (he died in 1972), who I knew as a member of the Worshipful Company of Cloth-workers and part owner of Maidstone's famous 'Turkey Mill'. The following are the notes he sent me and I quote:

Development (of Portland Cement manufacture) began from about 1839. The principal founder at Snodland (Holborough) was William Lee, my great, great, Grand-father, who started business there as William Lee, Son & Company, about 1840. He prospered and had an only child, Miss Lee, an heiress, who married my great Grandfather, Harry Roberts, Captain RE at Chatham. They greatly improved and expanded the business.

After by-passing my Grandfather, W. H. Roberts, the business passed to my uncle, W. H. L. Roberts, who took over from his father when he retired from the Army (Royals) in about 1899. He worked hard to restore the fortunes of the concern and in 1912, after making many improvements, succeeded in selling out to the British Portland Cement Company for between fifty and sixty thousand pounds out of which he had to settle with his partner Sam Lee Smith. Part of the contract with British Portland was that he had to undertake *not* to go into the Cement Trade for ten years. In 1914 he rejoined the Army and served in the First World War. But he began to acquire agricultural land to the west of Holborough and the adjoining countryside, thus getting nearer to the clay; with his first-class knowledge of local geology and the subsoil he was convinced he had puchased land which comprised a natural ready mixed raw material (for the production of cement) and so it proved.

In 1922, with the help of friends and the remainder of the proceeds of the sale of the old works, he ordered the latest rotary kiln and accessories from Vickers. Sir Percy Girouard who had served in the Royal Engineers, advised him concerning the design for the new works which commenced to operate in 1923 and very soon were profitably making a very high quality cement. Two years later a public company was floated to operate the enterprise with a capital of about £150,000 which was fully subscribed. This became the 'Red Triangle' and something of a menace to the Associated Portland Cement Manufacturers so when W. L. H. Roberts died in 1928 the former's interest at Holborough were taken over by the latter company who considerably enlarged the works there.

THEY ALL LOOKED MIGHTY DECRUIT IN 1930

To what extent smuggling along the Medway may be classed as a trade is a matter of opinion but in the heyday of this activity at the end of the eighteenth century it certainly contributed substantially to the ill-gotten gains of many people. Much interesting information on this subject is to be found in a curious little pamphlet by a colourful Maidstone character, George Bishop, who not only founded a gin distillery in Bank Street but also twice served as Mayor of the town, in 1777 and again in 1786. The twenty-page-long pamphlet, carried the title 'OBSERVATIONS, REMARKS, and MEANS, to Prevent SMUGGLING' and is commented upon in my *A Third Kentish Patchwork*. His opening remarks sum up the position as he knew it:

The smugglers are a very powerful body, and can raise considerable sums of money on any occasion that offers to promote their interest; they boast of having disposed of large sums in order to prevent any hurt being done to their trade, at one time 3,000 l. was disposed of. So little care is taken to prevent smuggling that there is not one excise-officer at Sheerness, where, in the river Medway the revenue loses 50,000 l. per annum, and has done so for many years back, which trade has so far increased, as nearly all the spirits, wine, tea, tobacco, raisins, &c., consumed in that neighbourhood are smuggled and His Majesty's ships that lay there for break-waters are made use of for storehouses, and the people of the dockyard are the smugglers.

At a sessions held at Maidstone in Kent (a little time ago) seven . . . able young men, were convicted and ordered to serve His Majesty as sailors; by seeing the lieutenant they procured their enlargement, and are now employed following this illicit trade as before.

The lives of the Preventive Men must at times have been full of excitement and not without danger; sometimes the result of their endeavours were unfortunate as the following news item from the *Kentish Gazette* of June the 8th, 1771, shows:

Last Tuesday a vessel appeared off Margate bound from Dunkirk to Chatham laden with rags. An Excise Officer, having ignorantly boarded her, was informed by the Captain that he must bear him company during the performance of his quarantine, but the officer choosing to refer to a better authority, returned to shore and applied to the Customs-house Officer to know if the Act of Parliament remained still in force. The commendable mortification is better conceived than expressed when, we are informed, the officer and his assistants were directed to return to the vessel and continue there during her quarantine!—A number of the inhabitants assembled on the Pier, upon this occasion, to behold the dejected quarantiners receiving from the sorrowful wives the necessary apparel, etc., for the time of their banishment.—The Next morning the vessel sailed for Stangate Creek.

The sequel came a month later when the paper reported on July 6th:

'On Thursday last the excise officer and his assistants who went on board a vessel in Margate Roads from Dunkirk landed at Margate Pier the month for their performing quarantine being expired; they looked very shocking, having been forced to lay on nothing but the boards; but in searching the vessel they found three

Teston Lock

The Palace and All Saints' Church, Maidstone
From a pencil drawing by E. H. Hills, 1831

Barges below the bridge, Maidstone

Photograph Maidstone Museum Collection

Waterside, Maidstone. An early morning study of the industrial
heart of the town, 1954

Aylesford Church and Bridge, 1829

Drawn by Bartlett, engraved by B. Winkles

A typical spritsail barge

Cuxton from Borstal, 1954

Shipping in the Limehouse Reach, Chatham

The Frindsbury Shore from the Bridge Beach, Rochester

Grain Oil Refinery

The London Stone, Upnor

Dredgermen at work about 1890

Rochester Admiralty Court, 1965

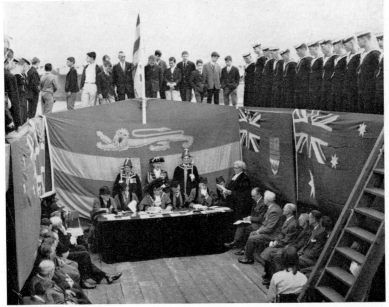

The Creek, Queenborough

The Medway at Garrison Point, Sheerness

tubs of Geneva concealed, therefore to revenge themselves on the Captain for his behaviour to them, they seized the vessel, and she is now ordered to Margate to be burned.'

In the past when that succulent bivalve the oyster was almost part of the staple diet of both rich and poor the lower reaches of the Medway, as well as the waters of the Swale and along the northern shore of Sheppey, were much used by the oyster dredger-men in their trade. I dealt with this subject at some length in *Archaeologia Cantiana* Vol. LXXX, 1965, but it may be appropriate here to give a short recap concerning the fisheries of Rochester, Queenborough and Minster-in-Sheppey.

Of the Rochester fishery Hasted wrote*:

the Oyster Fishery carried on in the several creeks and branches (of the Medway) within the liberties of this City (was operated by) a company of Free-dredgermen established by prescription time out of mind subject to the government and authority of the Mayor and Citizens.

The Rochester Corporation's jurisdiction extended from Hawkwood near Snodland to Sheerness and from medieval times Water Courts presided over by the Mayor were held at regular intervals on the river, even today the ceremonial of these occasions is re-enacted to keep the tradition alive. But the City of London claimed legal authority over the river as far as Upnor, the upper limit being marked by 'The London Stone' and fishing rights were a continual source of contention between the two authorities, in fact, as early as 1236 a number of the Medway fishermen were confined in Newgate prison following a brawl with their London counterparts.

By the 1860s the Rochester fishery was in a very bad state financially mainly through the loss of oyster brood occasioned by a series of severe winters, moreover, there was much pilfering of the beds by non-freemen. The extension of Chatham Dockyard at this time closed the oyster beds in Swinborough Creek whilst embankments along the river in many places had a similar effect so that by the first decade of the present century it became difficult to keep the industry going, and at the outbreak of war in 1914 there were only about twenty men and five or six boats employed.

* Fol. Ed. Vol. II. p. 22.

In his *Tour thro' Great Britain*, Daniel Defoe described Queenborough as 'a miserable dirty Fishing town—the chief traders . . . seem to be Ale-house keepers and oyster-catchers'. While the main activities of the Queenborough 'oyster-catchers'—cultivation and dredging—were no doubt directed to the waters of the Swale they must also have penetrated as far as the Medway saltings bordering Stangate Creek and the adjacent shores.

Despite the Edward III period castle it was not until the seventeenth century that Queenborough as a town grew to be a place of any size but when Hasted was writing his County History he was able to report 'that 120 or more "neat houses" lined the main street'! In an introductory note to his catalogue of the *Queenborough Borough Records*, Dr. Hull commented the town's 'main source of wealth until the nineteenth century lay in its oyster fishery'.

The Borough's jurisdiction over the fishery extended from the junction of the Medway and Swale to Kingsferry, but no doubt there was much surreptitious poaching of the creeks of the saltings outside this prescribed jurisdiction by the Queenborough men despite the opposition of the Rochester dredgers.

The opening years of the nineteenth century proved to be an unfortunate period for the fishery's finances and by 1815 debts amounting to some £9,000 had been incurred. These were covered by an issue of Corporation bonds but during the following five years the fishery accounts became over £14,500 'in the red'! During this period there was a continuing story of chicanery and double-dealing by those in authority, particularly by one of the jurats, Thomas Young Greet, who for some time filled the office of chamberlain and later became mayor. In 1820 the Mayor, Jurats and Bailiffs introduced new by-laws under which all the Free Dredgers had to register and could be fined if they failed to work at the normal tasks of cultivation of the oyster brood. These new rules led to great dissatisfaction and eight of the freemen filed a Bill of Complaint in the high court of the Chancery, the action later being carried to the Lent Assizes at Maidstone, in March 1822, part of the hearing being concerned with 'unlawful, riotous and tumultuous assembly', including an assault on the Mayor, Stephen Grestock, who had replaced Greet; the outcome was in favour of the Corporation.

Subsequently, Greet once more became mayor and held the office until 1828, but in the following year he died leaving the fishery concerns, which for so long he had dominated, in a thoroughly unsatisfactory state. More discontent followed. At a Court Leet the burgesses demanded that the corporation should produce the fishery accounts and when this was refused it became necessary to read the Riot Act. Eventually harmony was restored by an offer to the dredgermen of an extra shilling for every bushel of oysters gathered, but as Daly remarked in his *History of the Isle of Sheppey*, 'Great distress continued in Queenborough for several years afterwards; and tradition asserts that grass grew in the principal streets.'

At Minster the fishery was a quite small affair. The Alston muniments (Kent County Archives U 487 E 1) provides the information that this fishery belonged to the Manor of Minster and was comprised of twelve acres of fresh marsh called Scrape Hope: 'and the Oyster Ground and several fishing called Croggdeepe, otherwise Crockdeepe'. In 1701 a certain George Weston and six other fishermen took a seven years' lease of these grounds at an annual rent of £10. However, as time went on they were 'disturbed' by rival fishermen from the Medway and at the end of the term surrendered the lease. They were followed by another group which continued to stock and cultivate oysters in the 'Creeks, Dredging Grounds and places near the River Medway' encouraged by an interest-free loan from funds administered by the trustees of Sir John Hayward's Charity at Rochester which then possessed the manor.

In 1799, following a ruling by the Chancery Court, the trustees of the Hayward Charity sold the Minster manor to William Alston of Rochester, butcher and cow-keeper, and a James Payne. Then ten years later these two owners resold to Charles Wyatt but Alston retained the foreshore rights between Sheerness garrison and Serap(s) Gate, together with the Cheyney Rock Oyster ground.

William Alston and his descendants seem to have continued the fishery business for in 1847 Samuel Bagshaw recorded: 'The Cheyney Rock Oyster Fishery, extending from Garrison Point to Saunders Brook, a distance of 6 miles, is the property of T. D. and D. Alston', while Kelly's *Kent Directory* of 1907 states 'In front of the coast is the bank called "Cheyney Rock", which is an oyster ground', a statement which is repeated word for word in the 1938 edition.

An incalculable flow of water has passed down the Medway since the products of the wealden iron works, the ragstone quarries, fullers earth and agriculture found their way in modest vessels to the Thames estuary and so to the metropolis, the ports along the North Sea coast, and, more rarely, the nearer continental shores. But this traffic was not all one way and certain items of merchandise were imported into the country via the river. It comes as something of a surprise to learn that for some three hundred years one of the major sea routes to the West Indies has operated between Sheerness and Jamaica's Port Royal and, because of this link, for long Kent has been one of the distribution centres of the fruit which has meant so much to the West Indies prosperity—the banana. Today the Jamaica Banana Producers Steamship Company with fast modern refrigerated vessels maintain a weekly service from the island to the river mouth.

After the 1914–18 war, the first big impetus to the developing trade along the deep-water basin of the Lower Medway came when, in 1923, an oil refinery was established at the Isle-of-Grain to be followed in 1930 by the opening, further upstream, of the Berry Wiggins refinery. Then, in the early 1950's, the British Petroleum Company, realizing the value of this location, commenced the creation of the big refinery-complex with its ancillary wharfage which has resulted in the Medway becoming one of the great oil ports of Britain to which today supplies are carried in tankers of more than 100,000 tons burthen.

Upstream as far as Rochester, the ever-expanding use of the waterway for water-borne trade, and the increasing demand for berthing facilities at Sheerness after the second World War, has led to the establishment of the Medway Ports Authority, born out of the amalgamation of five statutory authorities, together with the Sheerness Harbour Company which previously had exercised control along the river.

A major project instigated by the new authority has been the construction of deep river berths and the general extension of docking facilities at Sheerness. Up-river the story has been the same, continual improvements to the many private wharves along the reaches to Rochester, a typical example being berth construction at Phoenix Wharf, Strood, being carried out at the time this is written.

In 1971 the *Kent Messenger* reported that up to December 31, 1970, 'the river handled 25,685,581 tons of cargo carried in 4,492 vessels, an increase of some 300,000 tons over the 1969 figures'. Today, with the country's growth of import and export trade, it is reasonable to assume that the tonnage being handled is considerably in excess of the 1970 figure so making the Lower Medway one of the most important ports in the south east of the country.

This then, but briefly sketched, has been the picture of man's use to carry his burdens along Kent's historic waterway from the days of pre-history when early settlers along the valley raised great sarsen stones to mark their presence and Roman invaders chose the river's beautiful banks as desirable localities for domestic settlement down the ages to our own noisy and hurried age when oil has replaced muscle and brawn or the power of the wind to propel craft through its buoyant waters.

2

A WATERINGBURY BELL-RINGER

HROUGH THE KINDNESS of a Wye resident, Mrs J. Haynes, I was given an opportunity of reading and copying some manuscript notes concerning Wateringbury and its parish church written by a certain Richard James Newman who was born and lived in the village in the earlier part of the nineteenth century.

The Newmans were a local family and intermittently, from April 1902 the *Kent Messenger* published a series of contributions under the title *Wateringbury Revisited: Or Fifty Years Ago*, written by a George Newman, whose father had worked as a gardener at 'the big house', Wateringbury Place, the home of the rich Mathias Prime Lucas, onetime Alterman of the City of London and always known to the locals as 'the Alderman'.

Richard James Newman must have been a relation although George Newman did not mention him in *Wateringbury Revisited* although he included details of various members of his family, his father, and his sister Mary Ann, who was lady's maid to the Alderman's daughter.

George was obviously better educated than Richard James for he had attended the village school, which had been erected in 1843 by Alderman Lucas as a *quid pro quo* for permission from the Dean and Chapter of Rochester to enclose a parcel of land at Canons Heath. In his autobiographical notes Richard James Newman included the following commentary on the subject. In this quotation, and the others which follow, the spelling, often phonetic, and complete lack of punctuation is preserved.

In 1830 in Doctor Marsham time when I went to Sunday School for there was no school At that time in Wateringbury till Mr

Stevens Came And had one built And he got the alderman Lucas to Build one And he did And they gave him sum ground on Canon Gath in Exchange And built the school for the poor   Canon Gath* belong to the poor of Wateringbury And to the Church to cut turf for the graves   there was a Stone in the Church that told you All A Bout it for I have Red it many A time And there was A Stone on the Gath when I Minded sheep and Cows up there so I think I ought to know A Bout it   Canon Gath is All in Wateringbury And Belongs to the poor   And I hope that you poor of Wateringbury have got As good A Sheperd As your Dear old Mr Steevens† was for he would not see his poor Baled out of there Birth Right nor his Church of her Rights   But a hungry Wolf will take any poor Man Sheep A way   And a hungry Man is the same   And I think you Wateringbury people Are a foolish lot of people to have your Birth Right took A way from you   But perhaps he will get Catched sum Day By a higher Lord then him   And whoes will Canon Gath Be then.

One of the manors of Wateringbury was Canons Court which, in the Middle Ages, formed part of the possessions of the Prior and Canons of Leeds, hence its name. At the dissolution, Henry VIII passed it by gift to the Dean and Chapter of Rochester, and in the eighteenth century the family of Style were tenants. In commencing his notes Richard James Newman wrote:

I Richard James Newman was Born in the parish of Wateringbury att a place called fulens Corner and I went to work at nine years old on Cannon Court farm for a Mr goodwen‡ for four pence a Day on Cannon Gath A Minding of Sheep and Cows And Cutting of Brakes for pecking of fruit   And there I worked over forty years.

Cannon Court is A very old place   When I was house Boy there use to Come A lot of old College Men And the Alderman Lucas And use to Read in it And then they use to have lunch   And then they went up on Cannon Gath And looked And then they went Back to the aldermans   A gain Cannon Gath is were thed used to Cut the turf for the Church yard when I was a boy and where the people use to cut wood to Burn in the Aldermans time   And there was a Stone in the Church that told you All A Bout Canon Gath I have Red it Many a time when I went to the Sunday School in

---

* Garth. An enclosure or yard.
† The Rev. Henry Stevens, M.A., eldest son of the Dean of Rochester.
‡ Goodwin and Wilcocks farmed at Wateringbury in the mid-nineteenth century. *Directory of Kent.* Bagshaw.

My grandfather time for he keep the Sundy School in Dockter Marsham time Before Mr Steevens Came to Wateringbury

In his 'Saunter Through Kent' series of books (Vol. XXII) Igglesden had this to say about Canon Court:

> Out of the opposite side of the village you follow a narrow road leading to Malling, leaving Wateringbury Park on your right, and you come to Canon Court, now a fine farmhouse surrounded by acres rich in fruit and hops. It is on the site of an ancient manor house, and during the reign of Henry the Third the estate was the property of Leeds Priory. Henry the Eighth, when he dissolved this and other religious houses, settled it upon his new institution known as the Dean and Chapter of Rochester. The North Pole Inn, so called from the cold blow up this way, stands in Canon Lane, at the top of which was once a common. I am told, however that the land was wrested from the parishioners several years ago.

Newman made a second reference to the subject about which he was much exercised, Canon Gath and its being 'wrested from the parishioners':

> ... it belongs to the poor of the parish and the Church not to Mr falmont (*sic*) nor his wife And there was A Stone in the Church that told you All A Bout it ... it was there when the Church was Altred (1886) And it ought to Ben put in A gain But no for it belong to the poor And that is the Reson it was forgot.

'There is' to quote Hasted* 'a vill or borough in this parish, containing the *west* division of it, which is called *Pizein-well* from one *Pizein*, who owned the well here. There was till of late years, a singular, though *a very ancient custom*, kept up, of electing a Deputy to the *Dumb Borsholder of Chart*, as it was called, claiming liberty over 15 houses in the precinct of *Pizein-well*; every householder of which was formerly obliged to pay the Keeper of this Borsholder 1d. yearly.

'This *Dumb Borsholder* was always first called at the *Court Leet* holden for the *Hundred of Twyford*, when its Keeper, who was always appointed by that court, held it up to his call, with a neckcloth or handkerchief put through the iron ring fixed at the top, and answered for it. This *Borsholder of Chart*, and the *Court*

* *History of Kent.* Fol. Ed. Vol. 11, p. 284.

20

The Dumb Borsholder in Wateringbury Church

A dipping well at Pizein Well, Wateringbury

The Thomas Crow sundial in the Churchyard

"Fulens Corner" before the "King's Head" was demolished

Leet has been discontinued about 50 years (i.e. about 1680); and the Borsholder, who is put in by the Quarter Sessions for *Wateringbury*, claims over the whole parish.

'This Dumb Borsholder is made of wood, about three feet and half an inch long, with an iron ring at the top, and four more by the sides, near the bottom, where it has a square iron spike fixed, four inches and a half long, to fix it in the ground, or on occasion to break open doors, &c. which was used to be done, without a warrant of any Justice, on suspicion of goods having been unlawfully come by, and concealed in any of these 15 houses.'

In his notes Richard James recorded his boyhood memories of the Dumb Borsholder:

'Now I will tell you A Bout the old Dumbosler when I was a Boy and went to the Sunday School I have played with it maney A time for it use to Be up in the Belfery And there was straps to it then And when A Mr feverstone came Counstable of the parish he wanted to take it out of the Church But My father would not let him for he was Sexton of the Church

'At that time And that was in the alderman time My father was sexten And a Bell Ringer sixty years And he was the Man that took the Dumbosler A way from feverstone And took it into the vestry Roome where it is now* Soloman Newman was the last one that used it for he was high Constible At ther time And Joseph Goodmen was Constible and Clark At that time

'Solemen Newman was last Man that used the Dumbosler in sixteen hundred and twenty five At pisen well and on Canon Gath for pisen well was A notorus place for smugling At that time This is Copied from one Solomanes Newman Book one of the oldest Bell Ringer family in England And Wateringbury is ther parish fer this last four hund(red) yeares this is Coped By Me Richard James Newman.'

The secluded hamlet of Pizein Well on the east side of the Mereworth Castle domain is reached by a by-road from the A26 or alternatively by the lane which branches south-west from the main highway opposite the parish church. The place lies in a hollow with a number of the older cottages standing on a bank and approached by flights of stone or brick steps. Water from the

---

* Today the dumb borsholder is hung on the wall above the archway leading into the nave from the south door.

string of lakes in Mereworth park finds its way, either above or below ground, through the area before it joins the Medway close to Wateringbury bridge. Brief diary notes of a visit I made to Pizein Well in July 1968 read: 'Found the secluded group of houses but most of the occupants were away; however at a cottage under repair the lady owner appeared; she had come to see the progress of the builder's work. In the back garden she showed (and allowed me to photograph) the picturesque dipping well which formerly, she informed me, was used by all the "locals". This was but one rise of the springs in the immediate vicinity.'

The origin of the place-name may have derived from early ownership of a person or family named Pizein, later the hamlet became known as Poison or Pizzen Well. In a *A Saunter Through Kent* (Vol. XXII), already referred to, Igglesden wrote:

I naturally enquired if a well existed, and there, plainly enough, stood a walled-in pool of water by the side of the road and directly opposite a row of cottages. It may be the upper part of a deep well, but the soil has silted up to such an extent that the clear water, enclosed by stones, is now but a shallow pool, fed by springs that apparently rise in an orchard close by. An old tradition is attached to the well, for we are told that if a young married woman wished for healthy offspring she must drink deeply of its water. In fact, wedding parties would walk to the spot and solemnly watch the ceremony of the bridegroom drawing water from the well and handing it to the bride. A strange old story, handed down through many generations.

When browsing through Richard James Newman's notes, so disjointed and repetitive, it becomes obvious that they were the jottings of an old man who in mind was becoming somewhat senile. Nevertheless as a human and local record they are not without value. His life interest was obviously in bell-ringing and his church and this is emphasized in the extracts (not quoted in the order written) which follow:

Soloman Newman was the last Man that used (the borsholder) for he was high Constible of the parish And he had six suns And all Born in the parish of Wateringbury. So you See dear friends that the Newmans Are A very old family of Bell Ringers And I Richard Newman have had 13 Born in the parish and Crisend At the old font where we all was And when My oldest sun was Crisned he had 5 grandfathers and 5 grandmothers (*sic*) so you see the Newmans Are A old famley Soloman Newman was 100 and 4 years old when he Died the oldest Bell Ringer in England he was high Constable 50 years at Wateringbury And he and his Suns Rung his last peel on the East Peckham Bells A peel called the London New Bob A peel of 700 and 20 Changes And the peel was Conducted By Soloman Newman there father the last peel he ever Rung.

I Richard James Newman A Bell Ringer for sixty years And I Rung the tenor Bell when I was oneley 15 years old And I have Rung in a Great Maney Bells in other Churches Besides Wateringbury And I have learnt A great many More to Ring in Wateringbury since 51 when there was a new peel of Bells put up By the inhabitants of the parish

And now Dear friends I will tell you who was the first Men that Rung the first peel on them on December the 31

John Seeds	the	1
William Newman		2
josech Bll (*sic*)		3
William Waller		4
Richard Baset		5
Richard Newman		

the peel was Led by John Seeds And Rung in 25 Minutes A peel caled the London New Bob A peel of Soloman Newman 700 20. Dear Friends this is the Blew Bells of Scootland Rung by Six Newmans At Saint John Church Wateringbury in 1864

O Where And o where is your iland laddy Gon
he is gon to fight the fowe for our King on our throne
And its All in My hart that I wish him Safe at Home

O where And o wher Did your hiland Lady Dwell
he Dwell in Merry Scootland Beside of the Blew Bell
And its All in My hart that I Love My lady well
Supose and Supose that your lighland lady should Dy
The Beg pipes should play over him I would set Me Down and
    Cry
And its All in My hart that I wish he May not Dy.

Newman's love of his parish church and its bells and his simple faith is reflected in the numerous references to both in his Notes, whilst several pages are devoted to epitaphs garnered from the churchyard, remembered and paraphrased.

I hope All the young people in Wateringbury will take Delight in the Church And Church yard As I have done for over 60 years.

Dear Friends whoe Read this Book go into Saint Johns Chruch yard and theare you will see A fine and Splended yew tree And A fine sun dill And sum old And Anchent toombes With in this Church yard side by side are Many A long low grave And som have Stones Set over them And on sum the green grass wave There is Maney A little Christon Child And we pass By them everry time that we go into prayer They cannot hear our foot steeps come They canot see us pas They canot feel the Bright warm sun that shines up on the grass They cannot hear when the great Bell is Ringing over head they cannot Rise and come to Church with us for they are Ded. But if we Believe that Christ shall Come then All the Ded shall Rise And they who sleep Down in there graves will open A gain their eyes for Christ our lord was Buried once He Died and Rose A gain He Conkred Death And left the grave And so will Criston men.

An oft-quoted epitaph to a Wateringbury blacksmith reads:

> My sledge and anvil I've declined;
> My bellows, too, have lost their wind;
> My fire's extinct, my forge decayed,
> And in the dust my vice is laid;
> My coals are spent, my iron's gone,
> My nails are drove, my work is done.

These lines are sometimes met with in parts of the country other than Kent. Newman gave as an alternative rendering:

> My hamer and My handvil,
> My fire and My tongs,
> My Belowes they have lost there wind,
> And now I must Decline,
> And look for A Beter home,
> A beter home to find.

> Death was no terror to him or surprise
> For 'is lamps were trimed and his light Burning.

and in another place:

> My hammer and sleg I now Decline
> My Felowes to have lost theare wind
> My handvill and My vice and Drill
> for want of strength they now are now still
> My fire is gon out My forge is Closed
> My nail is Drove and My work is done

Concerning the "fine sun Dill" Arthur Mee observed* it was made "in the 18th century by Thomas Crow. It has four dials, and shows noon in many cities, the months, the hours and Greenwich time", and Igglesden, "A famous native of Wateringbury was Thomas Crow who lived in Canon Lane and was the inventor of the Siemens octant, an instrument for measuring angles and generally called a quadrant. He died in the Tower of London and was buried in a vault in the churchyard." Newman's reference reads "Mr Richard Crow gave to the Church the Sun Dile the truest in England. That And the old Dumbosler And the old yewtree is the pride of the parish. The yew tree was planted in the year of 1500 and 97 By thomas Hoad on Janet the 2 in Remberance of his Brother."

Canon farm is the oldest farm in Wateringbury And had Been in the Bratles And good mens time a long Many years. In 1832 I was house Boy so I think I know a little A Bout it And he has Ben the Best Master in Wateringbury to his Men and Women and God will Reward him.
The Alderman Lucas Died January 1848
The sharpest frost that ever was known on the Record of Man was on the 23 of June 1851 As thich as a Shiling But Dear Friends there is nothing unpasable to the Lord.

The last page of the notebook found the old man still reminiscing in his wandering manner.

Before completing my exploration of Wateringbury I felt I must make a visit to Canon Court where Alderman Lucas and the "old College men" used to forgather and the Gath where Richard James as a boy was employed "a minding of sheep and cows and cutting of Brakes."

---

* *The King's England. Kent.* Hoddern & Stoughton 1936.

25

Some two hundred yards west of the churchyard a dead-end lane leads to the north past a number of small houses and cottages until, near its end, it reaches 'Little Canon' and 'Great Canon Court', a distance of nearly three-quarters-of-a-mile from the main road.

Canon Court stands back from the lane beyond the ancient farm buildings—a fine barn and stockyard. It is an attractive house of some age, probably eighteenth-century, which has been altered or added to since the Alderman's time, standing in a well-kept and colourful garden. Richard James Newman no doubt would have some difficulty in recognising the building and surroundings he knew, but the nearby great barn would have a familiar landmark to him. I was glad to have visited the spot with its long story of ecclesiastical and private ownership, a not unimportant facet of local history.

3

CROSSING THE ENGLISH CHANNEL IN 1840

IN SEPTEMBER 1840 a month-long tour through Belgium was undertaken by an invalid gentleman who suffered from a chest complaint accompanied by a friend. Upon his return the traveller, with much labour and care, wrote of his experiences in diary form, and the resulting bound volume came into my possession, by purchase from an antiquarian bookseller some years ago.

The work is unsigned, and the only indication of who the writer may have been is suggested by the armorial bookplate pasted on the inside of the binding which shows the arms of the Green family above the name 'Henry Green' who, from the heraldic evidence, was the second son of his father.

To judge from the two charming wash-drawings which decorate the diary pages—the small but elaborate initial letter with which the script opens and the plate entitled 'Beguines' (both illustrated here)—it may be inferred that Henry Green possessed a not inconsiderable artistic talent, but his name does not appear in Algernon Graves' *Dictionary of Artists 1750-1893*.

The long account of the various towns visited—Bruges, Ghent, Brussels, Louvain, Mechlin and Antwerp—is of more than passing interest, although at times somewhat pedestrian in character and with reliance on contemporary guide-book material, does not concern us here, but as a comment on travel conditions to and from the continent in the earlier part of the 19th century, the extracts which follow seem worth putting on record:

AMONG the various alterations which have taken place within the last twenty five years, there has not been one of more paramount importance than the improvement in our mode of travelling by sea as well as by land. As late as the year 1817, the communication between Dover and Calais was by sailing packets; at that time I expressed an opinion that ere long, they would be superseded by Steam boats; but the idea was laughed at;—such a thing was impossible. They have now been established some years,* and these few miles that not unusually occupied a space of ten hours, are now accomplished in a little more than a fifth part of that time. Nor is that the only advantage gained. At the period I speak of, the Dover Captains (there was a company of them) thought nothing of detaining their passengers for three or four days until they had amounted to a certain number, unless those who were waiting consented to pay an extra sum for sailing immediately. But to an invalid the change is most beneficial. In passing from London to Calais or Boulogne the voyage may be performed in comparative luxury; he need only lie down on one of the sofas which surround the "Saloon", and sleep, if "that be his wont"—if wakeful, he may read—if inclined to conversation, he is sure to find one or more inclined to kill time by the same means. With a view to regaining that health and strength which long illness had sadly impaired, I embarked (accompanied by Robt S Hayes) on board the City of London, Capt Grant, for Calais, and quitted the Adelaide Wharf at 10 minutes past 12. Having passed through the Pool, I quitted the deck, and ensconced myself in a comfortable corner of the Cabin, leaving the enjoyment of 'down River' scenery to those who might appreciate it. To me it is painfully monotonous, and I am in a measure grateful for any little incident which tends to rouse me from the listlessness it produces. A circumstance did occur, which, although it caused a hearty laugh at first, in the end called forth our earnest sympathy. We had got about ten miles below Gravesend, and had just sat down to dinner, when the mate made his appearance and acquainted the Captain that there was a lady on Deck who 'wished to be put ashore at Gravesend'.

---

* It was in 1815 that the first steamship line came into service on British waters covering the run from Liverpool to Glasgow. Eleven years later, what then was considered an exceptionally large vessel, the *United Kingdom*, was launched for the trade between London and Edinburgh, the year after the General Steam Navigation Company was floated although its charter of incorporation was not granted until 1831. The Company's intention was to provide shipping services in all the waters around Great Britain including the passenger trade from London to Margate; later this was extended to nearby ports across the Channel. The *City of London*, in which Robert S. Hayes and the diarist made the journey to Calais in September 1840, was a General Steam Navigation Company vessel.

Initial Letter on
the first page of
the Diary.
A wash drawing

**A Wash Drawing presumably by
Henry Green**

Béguines. (from Memory).

The arrival at Dover on the 6th February, 1840, of Prince
Albert of Saxe-Coburg
Engraved by W. Miller after the painting by W. A. Knell

Dover Harbour, 1831
Engraved by A. Prior after the painting by George Chambers

'Give my compliments to the Lady', says our skipper, 'and tell her that I will put her on shore there on Monday, as we return from Calais where we are now bound.'

Upon inquiry her situation proved to be most painful; she had been put on board in the belief that it was the Gravesend boat, and being an entire stranger, she never dreamed of asking any questions until the moment just mentioned. She had left London to go to Maidstone for the purpose of attending the funeral of a Sister who was to be buried that afternoon, some of her family being at Gravesend in waiting for the boat, and to conduct her to the former place.

On hearing her tale, the Captain resolved on putting into Margate for the purpose of landing the poor mourner, and sending her to his own residence there* with a letter of introduction to his wife, requesting that she might receive every care and attention. A director of the Herne Bay Steam Boat Company, who chanced to be on board, was not to be outdone by our kind-hearted Captain; he supplied her with an order for a free passage from thence to Gravesend.

By 10 o'clock in the evening we were off Calais pier, but had to wait three quarters of an hour before there was sufficient depth of water to enable us to enter the harbour. By a quarter past 11 we were enjoying a hot supper at Robert's Hotel, having cleared such part of our baggage as was required for immediate use.

An early description of the Herne Bay Steam Boat Company and the pier is to be found in Bagshaw's Directory.

The Royal Pier, which stretches imposingly into the bosom of the water, was commenced in the year 1831 by the Herne Bay Company, which was incorporated by Act of Parliament 1st of William IV. The amount raised was £50,000, in shares of £50 each. Its extreme length from the shore to the sea is 3,000 feet, and the width 24 feet. A sailing carriage runs upon iron grooves in the centre of the pier, for the purpose of conveying passengers and their luggage to and from the steamers.

The noble steamers embark passengers every day during the season, and every alternate day during the winter months. Omnibuses are daily in attendance to convey passengers to Canterbury, Dover, Margate, Ramsgate, etc.

The following morning the two travellers retrieved the remainder of their belongings, however not without some frustration.

* In 1847 a John Grant, gent. lived at Prospect Place. Bagshaw's Directory.

HERNE BAY FROM THE SEA.

Whilst at breakfast the Commissioner brought our passport duly viséd, and the keys of the baggage, all of which had been cleared; his demand was one franc, which with two francs for his trouble, was cheerfully paid, Having discharged our Bill at the hotel, we betook ourselves to the massagerie from whence we were to start per diligence for Dunkerque, when a Gentleman came up to me, announcing himself as Commissioner for Baggage, and politely demanded three francs—one for passing the baggage—two for porterage—and 'whatever I pleased for himself', hinting that, as a small carpet bag had been cleared the night before, his expecta-tions amounted to two francs more, which I accordingly paid, but I lament to add, not with that equanimity of temper which my friend Brockendon so strongly recommends in his guide book to Italy.

This was the first of similar extortions which punctuated the journey of Henry Green and Robert Hayes through Belgium, but the incident pales into insignificance compared with the reception

they met when a month later they returned to Dover. The diary
entry for Thursday, 24th September, gives the story.

Having to start by the diligence this morning, at ½ past six we
desired to be called at 5 in order that we might have breakfast before
we left. By carelessness or accident we were not called until 6, and
then I had merely time to dress myself, and set off to reach the office
as well as I could. My breathing this morning was if possible more
painful than ever, and it was only with great exertion I could reach
the Bureau a quarter of an hour after the time appointed, but luckily,
still in time for the diligence. I was so completely exhausted that some
time elapsed before I recovered. We journeyed through Gravelines,
and arrived at Calais in four hours and a half; we learned that a
packet was to leave at 12 for Dover, and therefore took every
precaution relative to Passport and luggage, to enable us to make
our passage by her. We ordered some refreshment, and by the time
the Commissioner of the Boat (!) made his appearance, we had
satisfied our appetites, paid our Bill, satisfied the Commissioner of
the Inn (!) and were ready to go on board.

I have no love for Calais, nor its extortions. In this opinion I am
not singular, nor is the idea of recent origin. In the reign of James
the 1st an author thus writes his feelings regarding Calais, as
'a beggarly extorting town, monstrous dear and sluttish'. That the
former part of its character is kept up, there can be no doubt, but
it is equally true that since the year 1818, when I first saw it, rapid
and essential improvements have been made in the town.

At ½ past 1 o'clock we moved from the pier, and in ten minutes
time had cleared its whole length. In three hours and a quarter
from our starting, we found ourselves anchored in Dover harbour,
for unfortunately the tide would not serve for our getting into the
pier. We therefore had no choice but landing by boat, and then
commenced a system of Extortion, to which that on the opposite side
would not compare. It was hoped 'that we would not object to pay
four shillings each for landing us'. Vain hope! for I did object most
decidedly doing anything of the kind, with a hint at the same time
of leaving it to the Mayor to decide the point. This brought them
down to the permitted charge of 2/6, accompanied by a hope that
I would give them something for the luggage. That was declined—
the boat grazed on the shingle, a board was placed, over which we
walked, for which the modest demand of one shilling was made and
satisfied.

Then came the crowd of Commissioners ready to tear us in pieces
(for we were the only passengers) enumerating the various excellent

qualities of the different hotels, and the conveyances therefrom to London. By the interference of the Police, and on the assurance that I would not go to any one of the hotels so recommended, an avenue was made, and we gained the top of the beach. Here a portion of these hornets followed, to watch our movements, nor did they quit us until we arrived at the Dover Castle Inn. The Commissioner attended us to the Custom house, close by, to clear the luggage which was accomplished in about five minutes. It was conveyed to the Inn (one trunk and a hat box) for the moderate sum of half a Crown, and one shilling to the Commissioner for his trouble! making in all, nine shillings and sixpence for landing and baggage. Let us not after this accuse our French neighbours of extortion.

This subject of exorbitant tolls and fares demanded by the Dover watermen for bringing passengers on shore when the state of the tide prevented the 'Packet Boat' getting alongside the north or south piers of the tidal harbour is touched upon by Rixon Bucknall in his *Boat Trains and Channel Packets*.*

As there was no means of escaping from Dover until the next morning, we secured beds, and after enjoying some really good tea, accompanied by some equally good broiled ham, we retired for the night, which was so stormy that our prospect for the next morning's ride was but gloomy. To prevent the chance of delay, the bill was ordered, so that breakfast only was added, in the event of our taking such a meal.

Friday, 25th September. We had secured our places over night for Herne Bay, and having sufficient time, partook of some breakfast; the Bill was brought, but the breakfast not being included, the waiter took it out for the addition to be made, and on presenting it, I found, to my utter surprize, they had altered the charge for beds, of course increasing it. This was the finishing stroke, and the annoyance was increased from the circumstance of my being known as an old customer to the house. I paid the demand, giving my hostess to understand that she had seen me for the last time as an inmate of the Dover Castle Inn.

At 7 o'clock we quitted the headquarters of extortion, for such is Dover, and arrived at Herne Bay a little before 11. A kind of omnibus, running on rails, was waiting at the gate of the pier, and in this machine, propelled by half a dozen men, I was conveyed to the further end, for two pence. In a few minutes we started, and as the

* Vincent Stuart Publishers Limited 1957.

clock struck 5, we landed at the Adelaide wharf, London Bridge. Another hour, and we were safely arrived at my own comfortable home, after an absence of twenty eight days.

Should an Englishman wish to know the real meaning of that 'untranslatable' word 'home', let him travel abroad, and on his return he will then appreciate its full value and meaning. In making this remark, let me not be misunderstood. During my absence I have seen much to gratify the most fastidious taste—I have experienced the warmest kindness from Strangers—I have met with many real comforts—and perhaps as few annoyances as must fall to the lot of every traveller. But though thus fortunate, absence only increased my love of home; a feeling considerably inceased by warmth of reception.

It is impossible not to be impressed by the thought and labour entailed in producing this beautifully inscribed account with its clear copperplate calligraphy, each line finishing to provide a perfect right-hand margin, every page numbered and appropriately headed and a long appendix section providing a list of placed visited, time occupied in travelling and distances; eighteen pages are devoted to 'Travelling Expences' and twenty-four to an Index.

To complete this account of crossing the English Channel in the 1840s—in such vivid contrast to modern-day conditions, when a journey by hovercraft from East Kent to France can be made in barely thirty minutes—it may be of interest to quote the relative entries of daily expenditure, although it is not made clear whether the friend, Robert S. Hayes, paid his own way or was the writer's guest.

Travelling Expences.

		£	s	d
Saturday 29th Aug:	Fare to Calais	1.	10.	–
	Cabriolet		4.	6
	Dinners		7.	6
	Calais. Roberts' Hotel	Fr:		Cts
	Supper	4		
	Cognac	1		5
	Beds	4		
	Servants	3		35

33

		£	s	d
Sunday 30 Aug:	Breakfast		4	
	Curaeva			10
	Servants		3	
	Passport & Comm		3	
	Luggage & Comm		5	
Thursday 24 Sept.	Breakfast		3	
	Servants			15
	Diligence to Calais		11	
	Luggage		1	
	Dinner		3	
	Brandy		1	5
	Servants		1	45
	Cigars		1	
	Passport & Permit		1	
	Luggage, porterage			50
	Commissioners		1	
	Comm^r of Boat		1	

		£	s	d
	Passage, Calais to Dover		11	
	Boat for landing		5	
	Landing from boat		1	
	Luggage, Custom House		2	6
	Commissioner		1	
	Tea and meat		4	
	Negus		3	
	Beds		3	6
	Servants		2	6
Friday 25 Sep:	Breakfast		3	
	Servants		1	
	Coach, Herne Bay		9	
	Pier and Luggage		1	
	Steam Boat to London		13	
	Dinner		6	10
	Porterage		9	
	Cabriolet		4	6

The diarist was obviously proud of his work for the folios of writing were handsomely bound in brown tooled leather with gilt embellishments—the lettering on the spine and round the edges of the binding and the paper—in short, worthy treatment for a labour of love.

4

NORMAN DOORWAYS

Y SCHOOL DAYS were spent within the shadow of Canterbury Cathedral. Originally founded by St. Augustine in 597 a disastrous fire in 1067 destroyed most of the Saxon building and when in 1070 Lanfranc, Abbot of Caen in Normandy, was consecrated Archbishop, a start was made to replace the ruined fabric and the monastic buildings, adopting the Romanesque architectural style used for the Abbey churches of Northern France. The work was continued by Lanfranc's successor, Anselm, his prior, Ernulf, and later Conrad, resulting in a magnificent Norman building.

In a Canterbury environment it is perhaps hardly surprising that I should have developed a love for the strong and bold style of our native Norman architecture, which, following its introduction to this country, was quickly adopted for all church building activities, monastic or parish, throughout East and Mid-Kent.

The story is the same for the Rochester diocese. Encouraged by Lanfranc the building of the Norman cathedral church and the Benedictine priory of St Andrew was commenced by Bishop Gundulph about 1080. By 1140 most of the nave had been raised while the striking west front, with its remarkable doorway, a façade seemingly based on prototypes at Poitiers,* and western France was completed twenty years later.

It is likely that much of the work was carried out by French masons who helped to train their English counterparts in their craft, and the skill the latter acquired spread to all parts of the diocese where the rebuilding of Saxon churches in the Romanesque

---

* The west front of Notre Dame la Garde.

35

manner was under way. Some of the French master masons may also have worked in East Kent for the doorway at Patrixbourne shows marked similarities to the details of the west front at Rochester.

During my school days I commenced to study architecture and to take photographs in and around Canterbury to illustrate the Norman and Gothic styles. One subject which I have always considered of particular interest I include here for it was one of the first photographs of an architectural subject that I took, I forget the precise date, probably it was 1905 when, in studying the subject my main guide was Parker's *An Introduction to Gothic Architecture*. This book, first published in 1849, which ran through numerous editions and became a standard work, contains a line-block illustration over the caption 'Part of Arcade, Canterbury. Shewing the junction of the old and new work' amplified by a description taken from the writings of Gervase, the monk, of the cathedral's reconstruction following the great fire of 1067 and contrasting the old and the new work. 'There (in the destroyed building) the arches and everything else was plain, *or sculptured with an axe and not a chisel*; but here; (in the new work) almost throughout, is appropriate sculpture.'

I searched for this record of the changing style at the turn of the 12th century—the A.D. 1110 Norman, worked with the axe, and the embryo Gothic of 1180 introducing the Early English dog-tooth enrichment worked with a chisel—and found it, part of the wall arcading, in the south aisle of the Choir. Some inspired monk, skilled as a mason, no doubt worked the right-hand arch as a guide to others of the coming architectural change. Today his work remains to help the uninitiated to date work of the period.

Norman Doors

It must have been about 1906 that I first visited Barfreston— by 'push-bike' from Canterbury, a distance of some ten miles, and so became acquainted with the small and remarkable church of St Nicholas called by one writer 'a text-book piece of Late-Norman architecture'. A few years later I made a second visit, this time armed with my ¼-plate 'Sanderson hand-and-stand' camera and made a photographic record of the building, particularly of the beautiful south doorway of the nave, a print from which is reproduced here. Then in the mid-twenties I carried out a close study of the church for a monograph which was published as No. 28 in the S.P.C.K. series of *Notes on Famous Churches and Abbeys*. This diminutive pamphlet sold for the remarkable price of 2d! In it I remarked:

> "No records are known concerning the erection of the church, but during the extensive repairs carried out in 1840, which were necessary owing to the ruinous condition of the fabric, it became apparent that much, if not all, of the stonework was prepared for and built into some other building prior to being used at Barfreston. The wrought stone had been brought from the quarries of Caen in Normandy and the occurrence of carved fragments of ashlar mixed in with the flint walling suggests that the materials were taken from some demolished building.

In *Archaeologia Cantiana*, Vol. XVI, R. C. Hussey advanced the theory that much of the wrought stonework may have come from Hackington where Baldwin, who succeeded to the See of Canterbury in 1185, planned to erect a new monastic establishment. The monks of Christ Church were bitterly opposed to the project, and when the Archbishop died in the Holy Land in 1190, the newly-raised chapel was demolished and the stone taken to Barfeston. G. A. T. Middleton, well known as an architectural authority in the early years of this century, pointed out that many details of the carving at Barfreston are almost identical with similar work at Laon in Northern France, perhaps an indication that the French masons working at Rochester were also employed at Hackington.

The richly carved south doorway to the Barfreston nave is a gem, one of the finest to be found anywhere else in England. Perhaps it represents an insertion into the original walling for the arch penetrates the string course and the range of earlier windows now blocked up. Although these have pointed arches they may well be contemporary with the adjoining semi-circular ones in the chancel wall, the mouldings of which are of the plain roll type. Were these latter introduced at the 1840 restoration?

The south door, with its series of recessed orders and elaborately carved tympanum above jambs of two orders, the two outer shafts being free-standing, the inner ones attached, all with delicately

Patrixbourne, author's pen drawing made about 1910

38

carved capitals, makes it among the most decorative of its type which has survived. Space will not allow a detailed description of all the carvings, a subject which has been dealt with at length in Ronald F. Jessup's *Kent* (The Little Guides) and more recently in John Newman's *The Buildings of England—North-East and East Kent*. Briefly however the outer voussoir stones of the arch contains fourteen medallions surrounded by circular borders of foliage, with grotesque representations of human figures which seem to represent the signs of the zodiac and seasonal labours. The second moulding shows twelve foliated compartments containing human figures with a smaller and similarly treated roll enclosing the tympanum which has as its central motive our Lord enthroned upon a cloud, surrounded by medallions displaying heads of saints and bishops, the whole intertwined with foliage and scroll work.

In addition to the main nave doorway there is a far less ornate priest's door, blocked up, in the south wall of the chancel, also a simple north doorway with shafted reveals.

Nearer to Canterbury and almost as splendid as Barfreston is the small, late-Norman church dating from *c.* 1160, at Patrixbourne, where is to be found another highly enriched doorway in the base of the tower which rises from the narrow south aisle, a doorway almost certainly the work of the 12th-century masons employed at Rochester.

The base of the tower is used as a porch and the flat-headed door, flanked by buttresses, is set below a steeply-pointed pediment which encloses a semicircular niche containing an Agnus Dei carving. The circular arched head is comprised of five orders with a label-moulding enriched with dogtooth, the whole encircling the tympanum showing Christ seated in a mandorla, the oval panel being surrounded by angels and creatures of the Apocalypse. The arch rises from double jamb shafts which have highly decorative capitals; in short, the doorway, to quote Glynne's words, is 'one of the richest doorways that is to be found'.

The central west doorway of Rochester Cathedral makes with Barfreston and Patrixbourne a trilogy of outstanding examples of 12th-century mason's craftmanship in Kent, the motifs introduced almost certainly being based on French prototypes. The five orders of voussoirs making up the massive arch which encloses the tympanum rise from a similar number of jamb-shafts having carved capitals. The second of these shafts from the door opening on each side are decorated respectively with column figures representing, on the left, Solomon, and on the right the Queen of Sheba, or alternatively, as suggested by Jessup*, Henry I and Matilda. The carving on the tympanum shows Christ in Majesty with, on either side, angels, symbolic renderings of the Evangelists and, along the lintel, the twelve Apostles. An interesting structural feature of this lintel is the use that has been made of joggle joints to prevent the eight heavy stones that carry the massive tympanum from sliding when fixed in position. Jessup also suggests† that both the lintol and tympanum once formed part of an earlier doorway, c. 1130.

Most of the medieval churches throughout Kent had their beginnings in the Norman period although some arose on Saxon sites and incorporated at least some fragments of the earlier buildings. But between the 13th- to 15th-centuries, many were partially or totally rebuilt, enlarged or materially altered in architectural character. Following the holocaust of the Black Death, the pestilence which decimated local populations and seriously reduced the number of available craftsmen, there came a resurgence of church building and during the 15th-century towers were either built new or rebuilt, generally at the western end of the nave. As a result, a considerable number of Norman doors, often no doubt fine examples, were swept away.

All told some fifty Kent churches retain doors of the Norman period although a number of these, particularly those on the north side, have their openings blocked by infilling masonry.

It is something of a surprise to discover that by far the greater number of surviving examples are in churches located south of the Medway—the Canterbury diocese area: north of the river— the Rochester diocese—and especially near to London, they are a rarity. One outstanding exception to this, however, is the west door of All Saints, Orpington, a church which almost certainly arose on Saxon foundations, although it is now incorporated as a sort of anti-chapel in a large modern building. This door, dating

* *The Little Guides. Kent.* Methuen.
† *Ibid.*

WALL ARCADING SOUTH CHOIR AISLE, CANTERBURY CATHEDRAL
The left arch *c.* 1110. The right arch *c.* 1180

DETAIL OF
THE SOUTH
DOORWAY,
BARFRESTON
Note the
massdial,
bottom
right-hand
corner

Author's
photograph
taken about
1908

SOUTH DOORWAY OF ST. NICHOLAS CHURCH, BARFRESTON

Author's photograph taken about 1908.

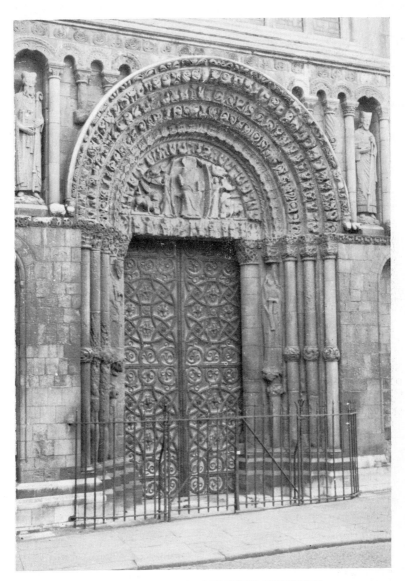

THE WEST DOORWAY, ROCHESTER CATHEDRAL

SOUTH DOORWAY,
ST. MARY MAGDALENE,
RUCKINGE

Below left:
WEST DOORWAY,
SS. PETER AND PAUL,
BORDEN

Below right:
WEST DOORWAY,
ST. JOHN BAPTIST,
BREDGAR

from about 1200, shows all the characteristics of Transitional Norman work, a pointed arch richly moulded and decorated with dogtooth and big undercut zigzag ornament, rising from two orders of shafts. Unfortunately, being within the west porch lack of light makes it difficult to fully appreciate the details.

The following is a list of Kent churches where Norman doors or their remains may be found:

Bapchild.
Barfreston. Magnificent S. door to nave. Plainer N. door.
        Blocked-up priests' door S. of chancel.
Bekesbourne. N. doorway to nave.
Betteshanger. N. and S. doorways to nave.
Bishopsbourne. N. doorway.

NORTH DOORWAY, BEKESBOURNE.
1815 print from *The Antiquarian Library*

Borden. W. doorway.

Brabourne. W. doorway. N. doorway to chancel.

Bredgar. W. doorway, reset.

Bridge. W. doorway with tympanum in nave. Doorway (reset) in N. transept.

Brook. An almost complete Early Norman church. W. and S. doorways, blocked.

Burmarsh. S. doorway to nave.

Chatham. S. doorway to nave.

Chislet. Blocked doorway S. side of central Norman tower.

Dartford. N. and S. doorways of tower. *c.* 1070.

Davington. Elaborate W. doorway, also (Cloister) doorway.

Dymchurch. S. chancel and W. doorways.

Eastry. W. doorway.

Eastling. W. doorway within porch.

Eynsford. W. doorway.

Hackington (St. Stephen's, Canterbury) N. door to nave.

Harbledown. W. doorway.

Hartley. (South of Gravesend) S. doorway to nave.

Hawkinge. W. doorway.

Hythe. (West doorway of transept).

Luddenham. (Near Faversham) W. doorway.

Lydden. S. doorway to nave.

Mersham. S. doorway (plain).

Monks Horton Priory. Doorway to church nave remains built in to domestic work of 1536.

Northbourne. N. and S. doorways.

Norton. N. doorway.

Orpington. Transitional Norman N. doorway.

Ospringe. Doorways N. side of chancel and N. aisle.

Paddlesworth (East Kent). N. and S. doorways.

Patrixbourne. S. doorway.

Romney. New W. doorway at the base of the fine Norman tower.

Ruckinge. S. doorway.

St. Margaret-at-Cliffe. W. doorway with pediment. S. doorway richly moulded.

Saltwood. S. and W. doorways.

Sandwich, St. Clement's. Small doorway leading to staircase turret at NW. angle of the central Norman tower.

Sellinge. W. doorway.

Smeeth. N. and S. doorways.

ST. MARGARET-AT-CLIFFE

Stoke. W. doorway.
Stone, near Dartford. Trans. Norman N. doorway.
Sutton by Dover. N. doorway.
Temple Ewell, near Kearsney. N. doorway.
Throwley. W. doorway.
Tilminstone. S. doorway with tympanum.
Walmer. St Mary Old Church, S. doorway.
Worth. N. doorway to nave (modern tympanum).
Wychling. Simple N. doorway (blocked).

Doorways of plain Norman design are also to be found in secular buildings such as the great castles raised after the Conquest (Rochester for example), and probably also in the more modest ancillary stone-built structures, even in domestic work, although in Kent none such examples survive, certainly nothing to compare with the Jew's House, Ipswich.

5

HUNTING, SHOOTING AND FISHING

HOSE who have the curiosity and time to browse through the files of early newspapers such as *The Kentish Post and Canterbury News Letter*, the *Kentish Gazette* or *The Maidstone Journal*—to name but three—will find that here and there are included as news or in the form of advertisements items concerned with the sporting life of the county which make fascinating and at times amusing reading. In the first volume of this *Patchwork* series I recorded a number of such extracts covering various aspects of local daily life of the period, but here the extracts which follow fall broadly within the above title heading. Unfortunately, limitations of space prevent more than a selected few being included—to cover the subject fully through the long period since local newspapers first appeared, would be an impossible task.

Throughout the centuries poaching has always been a perennial source of annoyance and loss to the owners of landed estates who in retaliation often made use of the Press to issue warnings to the malefactors concerned. For example, on August 19, 1769, the *Kentish Gazette* printed the following announcement:

WHEREAS the Game on the Manor belonging to the Right. Hon. Lord Bolingbroke, lying between Canterbury and Whitstable, and places adjacent, has for years past been destroyed by a parcel of people, not qualified, who live by the sale of it. His Lordship is therefore determined to prosecute all such who hunt, shoot or kill Game on the said Manor, contrary to Law. And in order to bring to justice those who offend, a Reward of Three Guineas will be given for every person so convicted; and Four Guineas for William Spencer of the City of Canterbury, as no Pains will be wanting in apprehending him, nor Expence spared in his Prosecution.—It is hoped that all Sportsmen will endeavour to bring such Persons to Justice, as the only Means of increasing their Diversion.

WILLIAM BELFORD,
Game-keeper to the above Manor.

When apprehended poachers were duly dealt with by the Courts:
On January 21, 1814, the *Kentish Gazette* printed:

Caution to Poachers.—Edward Webb, of the parish of Barham, was yesterday convicted before the Rev. Cooper Willyams, in the penalty of *ten pounds* for shooting hares in the night.

and again on June 7, 1814:

James Harlow, residing in the parish of Ash, was lately convicted before E. Boys, esq., one of the magistrates of this county, for having in his possession a hare, which he had shot, and fined the sum of £5, being the mitigated penalty for that offence under the Act of Parliament for the preservation of game, half of which sum was given to the informer, and the remainder for the poor of the parish.

The corn harvest of 1814 was seriously delayed by a summer of bad weather. The *Kentish Gazette*'s monthly agricultural report for September noted:

There is a vast breadth of corn upon the ground, but the coldness of the spring and the vicissitudes of the season since, together with the general defect of solar heat, must greatly have affected both the quality and the quantity. The sudden heavy rains also, and windy weather, have beaten down nearly all the weak, small, and thickly planted wheat. From a general concurrence, it is presumed that, should the weather continue favourable, the wheat crop may yet prove average; but all agree it must be inferior, in productiveness, to the crops of the years 1812 and 1813.

Because of this late harvest, landowners found it necessary to warn sportsmen to keep away from their estates. A number of advertisements to this effect appeared in the papers; for example, on August 30, the Earl of Guilford inserted the following announcement in the *Kentish Gazette*:

NOTICE

The Game on my several Manors and Farms, of Waldershare, Coldred, Popeshall, Linaker Court, in Whitfield, East Langdon, Guston Frith, North Court, and Boyton, in Swingfield, Beer, Monkton Court, and Park End, in Eythorne, and of Barville, in Tilminstone, and Napchester and Minaker, in Northbourne, and in all my woods will be strictly preserved. All persons are therefore warned from sporting thereon. And if any persons be found sporting upon any of them after this notice, they will be prosecuted according to law.

GUILFORD
Waldershare, August 25, 1814.

A week later Robert Hinde, Steward of the Manor of Milton, similarly advertised.

MANOR OF MILTON

NOTICE is hereby given, that in consequence of the backward state of the Harvest, all persons are requested not to hunt or shoot on the said Manor, extending over the several parishes of Bobbing, Borden, Bapchild, Bredgar, Hartlip, Halstow, Iwade, Milton, Murston, Milstead, Newington, Rodmersham, Rainham, Sittingbourne, Stockbury, Tonge, Tunstall, Upchurch, Minster in Sheppey, Eastchurch, Warden and Leysdown, until the fourteenth day of September.

ROBERT HINDE, Steward
Milton, August 29, 1814.

An advertisement in similar terms and headed 'GAME' was inserted in the same issue of the paper by John May in respect of 'such part of my Manor of Oxney as lies on the left of the Turnpike Road leading from Deal to Dover.' On account of the lateness of the harvest all persons were requested to 'refrain from shooting, coursing or sporting thereon . . . until after the 18th of September'.

The paper also carried an editorial comment:

GAME IN THANET.—We are desired to state, that from the unusual backwardness of the present Harvest, a number of gentle-men (sportsmen of Thanet), have come to a determination to defer the commencement of Partridge Shooting, until the 14th of Sept., and they particularly request those Gentlemen (inhabitants) who have not been consulted, and also all visitors in Thanet, to conform to their wishes on the present occasion.

The previous winter had been a hard one for on January 28 the *Kentish Gazette* offered the following advice:

It is strongly recommended to those gentlemen who wish to preserve their partridges, to lose no time in feeding them, as several coveys are known to have already perished from the want of this precaution, during the present inclemency of the weather.

Sudden death was no more a stranger to the early nineteenth-century than it is today, and from an editor's point of view always makes news, so that items recording such happenings are not uncommon in the columns of the local press. On Tuesday, June 12, 1804, the *Maidstone Journal* carried the following:

Yesterday se'night as Lieut-Colonel Hawker, with a party of his men, was fishing with a drag net, near Little Stone, in Romney Bay, on the ebbing of the tide, four of the men who held the extreme end of the net farthest into the sea, instantly sunk, and, notwithstanding they were all good swimmers, unfortunately never rose again.—It is conjectured they must have been drawn into a hole and swallowed up by the sand, as although every endeavour has been used as late as Wednesday morning, none of the bodies could be found, and it was then in contemplation to dig for them.

Less unusual—improperly handled firearms always have, and unhappily always will, lead to tragedy—the same paper reported on Tuesday, December 11:

Friday se'night between eleven and twelve o'clock, two young men being out shooting on the estate of Frederick Van Hagen, Esq., near Bexley Heath, in Kent, as one of them, whose name was John Fall, and whose parents reside at No. 11, Church Street, Newington, was going over a hedge, he placed his gun in such a direction that it unfortunately went off, and lodged the whole contents under the left jaw-bone, part of which penetrated through the head, and came out of the back part.

He was carried to the Golden Lion, at the corner of Bexley Heath, and never spoke afterwards. The Coroner's Jury sat on the body on Saturday and brought in their verdict—Accidental Death—John Fall was only fifteen years and a half old; his father belongs to the Custom-house, and the young man with him was a Clerk. He was shockingly disfigured.

On October 11, 1814, the *Kentish Gazette* reported a similar fatality:

On Thursday last, as John Barton, a young man a native of Bethersden, was shooting in a wood in that parish, and not being allowed to carry a gun, he endeavoured to conceal it on the approach of some person, when in thrusting it into some underwood for that purpose, with the butt end foremost, it went off, and lodged the contents in his side, which caused his death on the following morning.

Occasionally, such accidents were not fatal:

June 21, 1784

On Wednesday afternoon as Mr. Stephen Browning, of Whitstable, was off in a boat shooting wildfowl, his gun burst and blew one of his hands off.

Before the days of quarantine restrictions hydrophobia was an unpleasant danger:

February 8.

The following case of hydrophobia, which occurred in the parish of Bapchild last week, is considered extraordinary at this inclement season: On Monday evening a servant, in going to feed his master's dogs, observed a small tan-coloured beagle dog follow him into the stable, which immediately seized a beagle bitch. The man reported the circumstance to his master, observing, that the dog seemed strange. It was in consequence confined with a chain, biting everything offered to him, and particularly the chain, which however was not considered of moment, as dogs unused to be tied up are apt to do so. The dog being in very fine condition, was kept without food till Wednesday, on a supposition, that if he was sane he would eat when victuals were offered to him; but on barley meal being tendered to him, he refused it, and died on Thursday night. The dogs that were in the stable with him have since been killed; but, we are sorry to learn, that several dogs, which were bitten in

Bapchild-street, are yet at large; and, it is asked by our correspondent whether an action for damages would not lie against the owners, should any ill consequences arise from their neglect to destroy them? This is the second instance, in less than a year, of loss, from the same cause, at the above house. In the former, a pointer entered an out-house, where a brace of setters were chained up, which he bit, and they were in consequence killed. This dog appeared melancholy, shy and sleepy; but, the appearance of the beagle above-mentioned was quite the reverse.

Kentish Gazette, March 11, 1808:

We are sorry to learn that there are two or three mad dogs who have made their appearance in Swalecliffe and Reculver and also in the villages adjacent. Mr. R. Tassell has been under the necessity of killing three dogs that were bitten some time since, one of which seized a female servant by the apron, who, with great presence of mind, tore it off and escaped unhurt.

The papers from time to time reported on unusual natural history happenings, for example, on February 4, 1784, the *Kentish Gazette* noted:

Last Friday afternoon, between the hours of four and five, a gentleman walking from Hearn to Hoath heard a great noise at a great height in the air, and on looking upwards he perceived directly over him a flight of swans, he could plainly count twenty four. They flew not as wild geese, in the shape of a figure of seven or eight, but in a direct angle, steering their course towards Whit-stable, the Isle of Sheppey, or the coast of Essex. From the appearance of so many of these birds together in these parts, may we not have some reason to infer that they were driven from their own country by the severity of the weather, and much reason to dread, if former observations are to be depended upon, that a long continuation of frost may succeed their appearance here?

Maidstone Journal, February 2, 1802:

'The woodmen of Boxley Hill, zealous to imitate their superiors in the chase, on Saturday last turned out, at Upper Blue Bell, a marten cat, which had 15 minutes grace before it was pursued by three couple and a half of beagles. After affording an excellent run of two hours and a half, it was taken in a tree, with great difficulty; and we hear, this animal will be turned out again next Friday morning, on the same spot, when a number of sportsmen are expected to participate in this new and entertaining hunt.'

That marten-cats, no doubt of the 'Beech' variety, should have inhabited the North Downs woodlands as late as the nineteenth century is something of a surprise for writing in the 1860s J. G. Wood, in his well-known *Illustrated Natural History*, commented:

'The Martins are nearly banished from the more cultivated English counties, but still linger in some numbers among the more rocky and wooded portions of Great Britain.'

and continues:

'In Carnarvon and Merioneth they are still tolerably numerous, and are frequently hunted by hounds, as if they were foxes or other lawful game.'

Maidstone Journal, February 9, 1802:

On Friday se'night a bag fox was turned out at Ightham Common, before Mr. Simpson's harriers, of Fairlawn. He went away towards Seal, and took over the hills to Kingsdown, and on to Farningham; there he turned right, and went away for Ash, from thence to Grinstead Green; he then again took off to the right for Hartley, and on to Longfield, Meopham, Nursted, Shinglewell, Cobham, Shorn, and Gravesend, and was then taken alive at Milton near Mr. Gilby's, Denten, after a chase of between 50 and 60 miles; he had 20 minutes law.

Kentish Gazette, February 25, 1814:

FOX HUNT.—A most singular and pleasant fox chase took place at Malling, on Friday last, the 18th instant when Raynard was started from the bag at Fatherwell, and ran very reluctantly to the garden of a gentleman at Malling, from whence he ran to earth in a privy adjoining; on being released, the hunters did not think proper to suffer the nostrils of the cry to be offended with too much scent so turned him loose before some *puppies* which had never before hunted, who, after a good chivy, ran into him in fine stile; after which, another fox was turned out, and afforded good sport for two hours, when he ran to earth opposite the *Dumb Man's*, at the *Devil's own Child*, Upper Halling.

Kentish Gazette, June 21, 1814:

An extraordinary large Trout, of the Salmon species, was caught on Tuesday last in that branch of the River Stour, which passes through the Black Friars, in the centre of this City (Canterbury) by Mr. Linom. It measured in length from snout to tail, 2 feet 7 inches, in girth 1 foot 8 inches, and weighed 17 lbs. It had been observed in that part of the River for two years past, and it is supposed had been attracted there by the offal from a fellmonger's yard, in the vicinity.

The Kent papers, it would seem, were always glad to include in their Local News columns natural history items, even when they originated outside the county. One such appeared in the *Kentish Gazette* of October 14, 1814:

Last Tuesday a water fowl of a species totally unknown in this country, was shot in a pond belonging Mr. Stephen Grantham, at Stoneham near Lewes, where it had settled among some tame ducks. Its plumage is beautifully variegated, and the breast exhibits a spot, coloured exactly like the breast of a partridge, It measures across the back to the extremity of each wing, four feet seven inches, and from the bill to the tip of the tail, which is short, two feet four inches, and weighs five pounds fourteen ounces. Its wings appear especially formed for long flight, and the heads of both pinion bones are quite bear.

The above bird does not appear to have come under observation of any of the authors of natural history, except Berwick, who describes a bird nearly resembling the one in question, and calls it an Egyptian goose, but he at the same time confesses that he never could meet with one to enable him to give a drawing of it.

Two woodcocks were last week shot in the neighbourhood of Lewes.

On November 4, 1814, the *Kentish Gazette* carried the following report:

There never was such a quantity of fine new herrings known to be caught on the Kentish coast in the memory of the oldest inhabitant. Boats come in every morning so loaded, that they have been retailed in Margate and Ramsgate 33 for sixpence, to the great relief of the poor, and were it not for the great duty the poor have to pay for salt, it would afford them still greater aid of providing for the ensuing winter by pickling them. The red and white herring curers are allowed salt free of duty, which costs them only £5 per ton, or 5s. per bushell, whereas the poor, who want to use salt for the same purpose, must pay a duty on the same £25 per ton.

It comes as something of a surprise to learn that gun, game and dog licences are far from being a modern requirement. In August 1814 it was announced:

By an Act which received the Royal Assent on the 27th of July last, it is enacted, that such of the duties, provisions, and penalties contained in the Act of the 52nd of his present Majesty, as related so the persons aiding or assisting, or intending to aid, or assist, in the taking of any game, or any woodcock, snipe, quail, landrail, or coney, shall, severally cease and determine, provided the assistance given shall be done in the company or presence, of and for the use of another person, who has duly obtained a certificate to use his own dog, gun, &c. for taking and killing game, &c. and who shall not act by virtue of any deputation, or appointment.

As a result of this notice in its issue on Monday, September 12, the *Kentish Gazette* published the following:

KENT.—GAME CERTIFICATES FOR 1814.

An Alphabetical List of Persons who have taken out *Game Certificates* of *Three Guineas* and a *Half* each, in the County of Kent, made up to the Nineth day of September instant *Published* to an Act of Parliament, passed in the 52 year of the reign of King George the Third.

By Order of his Majesty's Commissioners for the Affairs of Taxes,
MATTHEW WINTER, Secretary.

For a number of reasons I have been prompted to reproduce the following long list of persons—over four hundred and fifty entries—with parishes of residence who applied for Game Certificates. Many of my readers will have some family connection with the County and those interested in their personal genealogy may find this century-and-a-half years old record of some value, particularly in relation to the parish of residence of the persons named.

There is interest too in the distinction drawn between 'the sheep and the goats', the 'esquires' who were the important people of the locality, often the owners of the local 'big house' and the others, many of whom may have been local farmers or at least involved in agriculture in one way or another. In this connection it would prove an informative occupation for those who can spare the time to consult a directory of the period to learn the calling and home address of the individuals named. In this respect Samuel Bagshaw's *History, Gazetteer and Directory of the County of Kent* (1847) to which I have frequently referred in the past, is a valuable source of information. For example to take one name at random—'Sawbridge, S. E., esq.' proves to have been Samuel E. Sawbridge, owner of the fine house and estate of Olantigh. Also it is surprising to learn how many parsons were addicted to the sport of shooting game. No doubt in many cases they and their families found such activity resulted in augmenting their larders to a welcome degree.

Names and Residence

Andrews, Ben, Stouting
Andrews, Thomas, Postling
Anderson, Mr., Seasalter
Ashby, Edw., Hackington
Abbott, James, Whitstable
Alley, George, Tunford
Abbott, John, St. Dunstan's
 (Canterbury)
Austen, John, esq., Cranbrook
Austen, J. T., esq., Cranbrook
Ayerst, Thos., Hawkhurst
Ayerst, Francis, jun., Hawkhurst
Ashbee, Rich., Pluckley
Ashburner, Rev. J., Linton
Archer, Clement, Ulcomb
Andrews, Rev. James,
 Boughton Monchelsea
Archer, Wm., Maidstone
Allen, John, Maidstone
Acton, Wm., Sutton Valence
Ash, W. W., Loose
Ayerst, John, Sutton Valence

Baker, Rev. Chas., Tilmanstone
Bridges, Sir B. W., bart.,
 Goodnestone

Names and Residence

Bushel, D. H., Ickham
Bing, Jarvis, Wickhambreux
Burridge, F. G., esq.,
 Hawkhurst
Barrow, James, Hawkhurst
Bishop, Samuel, Newenden
Bishop, Nicholas, Rolvenden
Bromley, Steph., Staplehurst
Britcher, J. M., Tenterden
Baldock, R. H., Seasalter
Baldock, W. H., esq., Petham
Baker, John, esq., M.P.
 St. Stephen's (Canterbury)
Bennett, Rev. Thos.,
 Christ Church (Canterbury)
Bennett, Rev. Wm.,
 Christ Church (Canterbury)
Brockman, J. D., esq.,
 Newington
Brockman, J., jun., esq.,
 Newington
Butch, John, Lympne
Bridger, John, Lympne
Barton, Hen., Hadlow
Barton, Walter, Hadlow
Bridger, John, Pembury

53

Names and Residence

Beale, Rich, jun., Biddenden
Beale, R., the younger,
                    Biddenden
Beale, Seaman, Biddenden
Baker, Thos., Cranbrook
Bonnick, Wm., Cranbrook
Beale, Seaman, Cranbrook
Bates, Isaac, Goudhurst
Bromley, Sam, Goudhurst
Barton, Boulden, High Halden
Barton, Thos., High Halden
Balmanno, Alex., Hawkhurst
Barrow, John, Hawkhurst
Beard, John, Loddington
Bradshaw, John, Maidstone
Best, T. F., Boughton Malherb
Best, James, Boxley
Bing, James, Stockbury
Bunnett, John, Lenham
Bing, Thos., Frinsted
Brice, Solomon, Frinsted
Bunnett, Thos., West Farleigh
Brattle, Robt., Wateringbury
Bishop, John, Hunton
Bishop, John, jun., Hunton
Boghurst, Philip, Ashford
Boghurst, John, Ashford
Barham, Rev. R. H., Ashford
Barten, Edw., Bethersden
Bullock, Rev. John, Little Chart
Bond, W. A., Great Chart
Butler, Thos., Ivychurch
Butler, Math., Ivychurch
Brett, Thos., esq., Wye
Burton, John, Folkestone

Coleman, Thos., Eythorne
Collard, Steph., Minster
Collard, David, Wickhambreux
Carter, George, jun.,
        St. Mildred (Canterbury)

Names and Residence

Collard, Henry, Longport
                    (Canterbury)
Callaway, John., jun.,
            Longport (Canterbury)
Collard, Robt., Hoath
Cantis, John, Hackington
                    (Canterbury)
Castle, Thos., sen., Folkestone
Castle, Thos., jun., Folkestone
Curling, Thos., Lympne
Cowel, John, Lympne
Cheesman, Thos., Brenchley
Corke, Ben, Tonbridge
Coveney, Thos., Benenden
Coveney, Thos., jun.,
                    Benenden
Collins, John, Goudhurst
Chapman, John, Hawkhurst
Cane, Robt., Hawkhurst
Cullen, Gilbee, Rolvenden
Collins, James, Sandhurst
Curteis, Robt., Tenterden
Curteis, Robt., jun., Tenterden
Curteis, George, Tenterden
Custeker, Edw., Ashford
Chamney, R. M., Ashford
Clarke, Wm., Ashford
Coleman, Edward, Dymchurch
Conrad, James, Mersham
Chapman, John, Westwell
Cotton, C. B., esq.,
                St. Peter's, Thanet
Cheesman, Wm., jun., Yalding
Cage, Rev. Chas., Bersted
Crouch, Thos., sen., Headcorn
Coulter, Daniel,
                Chart next Sutton
Coleman, Charles, Maidstone
Corral, Philip, Maidstone
Coulter, Henry, Langley
Cox, Robt., Lenham

Names and Residence

Cockburn, Rev. R., Boxley
Charlton, Thos., Loose
Curtis, T. H., esq., Ightham
Charlton, Steph., West Farleigh
Charlton, John, West Farleigh
Cheeseman, John, Hunton
Chilman, W., Wrotham
Chilman, John, Wrotham
Clarke, John, Yalding

D'Aeth, G. W. H., esq.,
                              Knowlton
De Chair, Rev. R. B.,
  Shebbertswold (Shepherdswell)
De Chair, Rev. John,
  Shebbertswold (Shepherdswell)
Denne, Hen., esq., Littleborne
Delmar, Charles, Elmstone
Delmar, Wm., esq., Petham
Dyason, Joseph, Hackington
                              (Canterbury)
Deedes, Wm., jun., esq.,
                              Saltwood
Delves, Henry, Speldhurst
Delves, Thomas, Tonbridge
Delves, Joseph, Tonbridge
Delves, Joseph, jun., Tonbridge
Durrant, J. M., Hawkhurst
Day, John, jun., Barming
Day, Thomas, Ulcomb
Dunning, W. A., Maidstone
Diamond, Joseph, Wateringbury
Deane, Thos., Winfield
Dudlow, John, West Malling

Elgar, Stephen, Wingham
Excell, Henry, Marden
Else, Rich., Bethersden
Ellis, James, Barming
Else, Edw., Lenham
Evelyn, Alex., esq., St. Clere

Names and Residence

Edmeads, Wm., Wrotham
Edmeads, Robt., Wrotham
Elvy, Francis, Yalding

Fox, Dan., jun., Barham
Fox, Wm., Nackington
Fowler, Wm., Elham
Friend, Rich., Lympne
Friend, John, Lympne
Fuggle, Thos., Brenchley
Forbes, R. W., esq., Rolvenden
Fisher, Thos., Tenterden
Fissenden, Peter, Chilham
Filmer, Robt.,
                    Boughton Monchelsea
Foster, James, East Farleigh
Foster, John, Lenham
Fuggles, John, Yalding
Foster, John, Yalding
Foster, Edw., Yalding
Friend, G. T., Birchington

Gibbs, Thos., Elmstone
Green, Wm., St. George
                              (Canterbury)
Gambrill, Thos., Stouting
Gordon, Rev. Wm., Tonbridge
Gordon, Rev. Wm., jun.,
                              Tonbridge
Gower, Thos., Biddenden
Gregson, Jesse, esq., Hawkhurst
Gladish, James, Marden
Gilbert, John, Marden
Gill, Rev. Joseph, Staplehurst
Greenhill, Rich., jun., Ashford
Golding, Thos., Loose
Golding, James, Barming
Geary, Sir Wm., bart., M.P.,
                              Oxenhoath
Gladish, John, Yalding
Gibbs, Rich., Yalding

Names and Residence   *Names and Residence*

Hamilton, Rev. James, Barham
Harvey, H. W., Eastry
Hopper, Robt., All Saint's
          (Canterbury)
Hopley, Sam., Tenterden
Hongham, Wm., esq.,
      Longport (Canterbury)
Horn, Henry, Hackington
Harvey, John, Petham
Honywood, Sir John C., bart.,
               Elmsted
Holman, Thos., Folkestone
Hubble, Thos., Capell
Hartridge, Math., Pembury
Huntly, Thos., Speldhurst
Hilder, John, jun., Tonbridge
Heath, Wm., Tonbridge
Hodges, T. L., esq., Benenden
Hague, John, Benenden
Hayes, Wm., Marden
Hardres, Matthew, Marden
Hichmott, Wm., jun., Marden
Hicknott, John, Marden
Hickmott, Thos., Marden
Hooker, Thos., esq., Marden
Harris, Wm., Rolvenden
Hatch, Robt., Ulcomb
Hodges, Dan., Ulcomb
Hollingworth, P., Thurnham
Head, Rev. Sir John, bart.,
      Boughton Monchelsea
Hollingworth, John, Loose
Hills, Wm., Boxley
Hills, Geo., Boxley
Hudson, Rich., Frindsbury
Hudson, Rich., Stockbury
Hartridge, Wm., East Farleigh
Harryman, Thos., Mereworth
Haffenden, Thos., Ashford
Haffenden, Wm., Bethersden
Harvey, Sam., Brabourne

Huckstep, John, Charing
Hatton, —., Eastwell
Hubbard, John, esq., Egerton
Hughes, W. M., Mersham
Howland, Geo., Warehorne
Howland, Wm., Warehorne
Holman, John, esq., Folkestone
Holman, Josh, esq., Folkestone
Hobday, Rich., esq., Folkestone
Hart, John, esq., Folkestone

Jennings, Anth., esq., Fordwich
Jones, Rich., Stanford
Joy, Robt., Brenchley
Johnson, Geo., jun., Goudhurst
Johnson, John, jun., Tenterden
Jeffery, Henry, Folkestone
Jemmett, Wm., Ashford
Jemmett, G. E., Ashford
Joachim, John, Lenham
Jennings, Geo., Dover
Jull, Thos., Wrotham
Jeffery, John, Yalding
Jeffery, T. W., Yalding

Kipping, Thos., Hadlow
Killick, John, Tonbridge
Knock, George, Charing
Knight, Edw., esq.,
          Godmersham
Knight, Edw., jun., esq.,
          Godmersham
Knight, G. T., esq.,
          Godmersham
Knachbull, Sir E., bart., M.P.,
          Mersham
Kennett, Wm., Wye
Kennett, Thos., Willesborough
Knight, W. B., esq., Folkestone
Kennard, David, East Farleigh
Knowles, John, Plaxtol

Names and Residence

Knowles, Wm., Basted
          (*sic* ?Brasted)
Knowles, Rich., Roughway

Lacy, Wm., Hoath
Lefevere, Steph., Marden
Lee, Wm., Maidstone
Lee, Josh, Ulcomb
Latham, John, Dover

Mackney, Thos., Sholden
Minter, Wm., Wingham
Matson, Charles, Wingham
Malborough, James, Seasalter
Montesquieu, Baron de, Bridge
Marsh, Richard, Folkestone
Milles, Wm., sen., Lympne
Milles, Rich., Lympne
Monckton, Steph., Brenchley
Marchant, T. B., Brenchley
Monckton, John, Brenchley
Monckton, John, jun., Brenchley
Mercer, Wm., jun., Brenchley
Mills, Thos., Capel
May, Walter, esq., Hadlow
Morland, W. A., esq.,
               Lamberhurst
Martin, Thos., Tonbridge
Moore, James, Biddenden
Mynn, Wm., Goudhurst
Morpheu, George, Tenterden
Murton, Geo., Charing
Morphett, John, Wittersham
Minter, Thos., esq., Folkestone
Mercer, Robt., Headcorn
Mercer, Thos., Headcorn
Malyn, John, Headcorn
Milner, Chas., esq., Preston Hall
Miller, John, Wouldham
Miller, John, West Farleigh
Miller, Rich., West Farleigh

Names and Residence

Mercer, Wm., Hunton
Mercer, Wm., jun., Hunton
Miller, Thos., Nettlested
Moore, Rev. Geo., Wrotham
Matthew, Thos., Wrotham
Miller, John, Yalding

Newport, George, Elmsted
Norton, Owen, Horsmonden
Neve, John, Halden
Norwood, C. Y., Ashford
Norton, Steph., Wrotham
Newton, Rev. D. H., Wrotham

Oxenden, H. C., esq., Barham
Oxenden, G. C., esq., Barham
Overy, Wm., Maidstone

Petley, Wm.,
          Ash next Sandwich
Petley, James,
          Ash next Sandwich
Prebble, Edw., Barham
Potter, Robt., Barham
Pembrook, Rich., Littleborne
Plumptre, John, esq., Frogham
Plumptre, J., esq., jun., Frogham
Percy, Hon. and Rev. Hugh,
              Bishopsborne
Plomer, Geo., esq., St. Mary
      Bredman (Canterbury)
Plomer, Geo. junr., St. Mary
      Bredman (Canterbury)
Packe, Chris, St. Peter
          (Canterbury)
Peckham, Rich., esq.,
           Bekesbourne
Pett, John, Hoath
Papillon, Thos., esq., Acrise
Porter, Michael, Hadlow
Powell, Baden, esq., Speldhurst

Names and Residence

Ponton, Thos., esq., Tonbridge
Pankhurst, Alex., Biddenden
Pix, John, Tenterden
Pilgram, Wm., Tenterden
Pomfret, Virgil, Tenterden
Pye, Thos., Charing
Payne, Wm., Crundale
Pope, Wm., Folkestone
Penfold, Steph., esq., Folkestone
Peale, Edw., Maidstone
Peale, John, Maidstone
Pope, D. B., Maidstone
Peene, Sam., Sutton Valence
Pierson, Rich., Wouldham
Philpott, John, West Farleigh
Paggitt, John, Winfield

Roberts, T. R. C., esq.,
              Cranbrook
Rugg, Geo., esq., Goudhurst
Rowlands, Rev. Wm., Halden
Richardson, Thos., jun.,
              Marden
Richardson, Thos., Rolvenden
Reynolds, Henry, Goodnestone
Rigden, John, Wingham
Rigden, Henry, Wingham
Rigden, George, Wingham
Rashbrook, Robt., esq.,
         St. George (Canterbury)
Rachell, John, Charing
Ring, George, Bethersden
Radcliff, Thos., Willesborough
Rachell, George, Chart Sutton
Romney, Right Hon. the Earl of
         The Mote, Bearsted

Swinford, John, Minster
Sankey, John, Barham
Simpson, Rev. Geo.,
         St. George (Canterbury)

Names and Residence

Simmons, Edw., Tenterden
Southee, Rich., Bekesbourne
Sawyer, Thos., Speldhurst
Saint, John, esq., Speldhurst
Scott, Thos., esq., Speldhurst
Serle, —., esq., Speldhurst
Sherlock, John, Tonbridge
Smith, James, esq., Tonbridge
Swatland, Steph., Cranbrook
Selby, Alex., Marden
Smith, Rich., jun., Rolvenden
Sedgwick, Thos., jun., Linton
Shidey, Sam., Chart next Sutton
Shidey, Wm., jun.,
           Chart next Sutton
Swain, Thos.,
           Boughton Monchelsea
Smyth, James, Chart Sutton
Smyth, Wm. Chart Sutton
Selby, George, Maidstone
Stacey, Courtney, Maidstone
Stacey, Edwin, Maidstone
Spratt, John, Stockbury
Summerfield, R. H., Aylesford
Starnes, L., Yalding
Stoddart, Rev. Charles, Ashford
Sayer, Rev. Geo., Charing
Sankey, Sam., Hastingleigh
Swaffer, Dan, jun., Kingsnorth
Stephens, John, Smarden
Sawbridge, S. E., esq., Wye
Simpson, Patrick, esq.,
              Folkestone

Tourney, Rev. Wm., Denton
Tomlin, F. A., Bishopbourn
Tickner, Thos., Rolvenden
Turner, Capt., Seasalter
Tassell, Mr., Seasalter
Tasswell, Wm., esq., Longport
              (Canterbury)

Names and Residence

Thorn, Francis, Brenchley
Twort, David, Horsmonden
Town, Philip, Goudhurst
Tapley, Daniel, Folkestone
Tomkin, John, jun.,
                    Chart next Sutton
Tyssen, G. W. D., Maidstone
Turner, Thos., esq., Hunton

Upton, Robt., Yalding
Ushmer, John, Egerton

Wright, Philip
          St. Mildred (Canterbury)
White, Wm.,
            St. Paul (Canterbury)
Wiltshire, Wm., Rolvenden
Ward, Edw., esq., Sandhurst
Witts, Edw., Tenterden
Waterman, Wm., Tenterden
Weller, Steph., jun., Tenterden
Weller, Steph., jun., Tenterden
Winser, Edw., Tenterden
Westfield, Robt., Elham
Watts, James, Brenchley
Waghorne, Joseph, Horsmonden
Woodgate, Hen., esq., Pembury
Worthington, J. E., esq.,
                      Speldhurst
West, J. E., Tonbridge
Woodgate, W. F., esq.,
                      Tonbridge
Witherden, Carey, Biddenden
Wilmshurst, Thos., Cranbrook

Names and Residence

Watts, Robt., esq., M.D.
                    Cranbrook
Weston, Henry, Goudhurst
Winch, Rich, jun., Hawkhurst
Winch, Wm., Hawkhurst
Wilson, Francis, esq., Hawkhurst
Winch, Benj., Hawkhurst
Walter, Steph., esq., Marden
Whitfield, Wm., Ashford
Witherden, Geo., esq.,
                    Bethersden
Weekes, James, Brabourn
Weekes, John, Brabourn
Walker, Robt., Wittersham
Webb, R. A., esq., Folkestone
Wilson, John, esq., Folkestone
Ward, Rich., Yalding
Wedd, Rich., Yalding
White, Sam, Yalding
Woollett, Thos., Yalding
Whitaker, Rich., Wrotham
Wooley, Wm., Ulcomb
Wise, B., Thurnham
Webb, Wm., Harrietsham
Webb, Rich., Harrietsham
Wodsworth, Rev. Chas.,
                    Maidstone
Wood, Wm., Loose
Whitting, Anth., Boxley
Winder, Thos., Lenham
Winder, John, Lenham
Webb, John, Harrietsham
Wimble, John, West Farleigh
Whitehead, John, Nettlested
Wood, Rev. R., Nettlested
Williams, John, West Malling

6

A VILLAGE SCHOOL

HEN the widowed Elizabeth Turner of Harrietsham Place, as the 'big house' of the parish was known then, died on the 25th February, 1783, the considerable property left by her husband, William Horsmonden Turner passed by his Will to Charles Booth, a great-grandson of Anthony Horsmonden.

By descent Charles Booth was connected with a number of important Wealden families. His grand-parents were George Booth of Marden and Ann Maplesden, daughter of Catherine and George Maplesden of 'Cheveney House', Marden, the grandmother having been a daughter of John Horsmonden of Goudhurst.

For several generations the Maplesdens had lived in Marden parish and Charles Booth's parents, in addition to the Cheveny House estate, owned property at Winchett Hill, Goudhurst, and 'Sprivers' in Horsmonden. When Charles Booth's great uncle, Edward Maplesden, died intestate in 1755, the family properties descended to his great uncle, Alexander Courthope, and himself as heirs in gavelkind; in consequence at the age of twenty he became a person of considerable wealth. Thirty years later, on the death of Mrs. Turner, his estate was very greatly augmented by the William Horsmonden Turner property at Harrietsham, Maidstone, and elsewhere.

In 1784 he was appointed High Sheriff for the County and received the honour of knighthood. Hasted described him as 'of the Temple, London', so it is reasonable to assume that he practised law as a profession. He did not marry until somewhat late in life, in fact, not until 1761 when he espoused Elizabeth, the widow of Edward Howell Shepherd, the son of Edward Shepherd, the architect/builder responsible for Shepherd's Market in Mayfair, the first Covent Garden theatre and many of the buildings on the north sides of Grosvenor and Cavendish Squares in London. Towards the end of his life, in addition to 'Harrietsham Place', Sir Charles Booth maintained a London dwelling No. 82 Charlotte Street, Rathbone Place. At Charlotte Street his neighbours included among others such well-known people in the art world as Joseph Farington, Richard Wilson, William Woollett, the Maidstone-born engraver, Richard Westall, and George Moreland.

Sir Charles Booth died on the 26th April, 1795, leaving a long and somewhat involved Will. In addition to various family bequests four sums were named to provide for the establishment of schools at Maidstone, Harrietsham, Horsmonden and Marden, places with which he had been closely associated. To Maidstone he left £2,000, Harrietsham £1,500, Horsmonden and Marden £1,000 each. Additionally to Harrietsham he left a further £500 for what has become known as 'The Bread Charity'—Booth's Charity for the Poor.

The Will concluded with a strange directive to his two trustees, Francis Ruddle and George Wade, described as Bankers and Stockbrokers of London,

'to make the best enquiry they can respecting my relations and kindred ... by Advertisement in the Public papers and otherwise to discover who are my relations and kindred and when they have obtained sufficient proof to satisfy their own minds who are my relations and kindred'

to distribute the residue of his estate among such persons giving

'the greatest share and proportion thereof unto such person or persons who in their opinion and Judgement shall appear to be my nearest relations and the most deserving ... well knowing and resting perfectly satisfied in the integrity honour and justice of my said Trustees.'

Obviously it is almost inconceivable that this worldly-wise testator did not in fact know who were his 'relations and kindred'. There is a tradition that Sir Charles was responsible for a number of natural offspring and rather than be involved in naming these he took the line of least resistance and left it to his trustees to sort out the tangle.

Of the bequest to Harrietsham the investment income on the £1,500 was to be used to providing a school-master and schoolmistress for the teaching of poor boys and girls from the Parish, whilst interest arising from the additional £500 was to be expended weekly on the purchase of bread to be distributed to such poor persons, resident in the Parish, selected by the Churchwardens and Overseers, who regularly attended Divine Service in the Parish Church. This Harrietsham 'Bread Charity' still operates.

Sir Charles Booth had directed in his Will that the trustees of the Harrietsham School should be the Rector of the Parish for the time being, the Owner of 'Harrietsham Place' for the time being, together with his executors Ruddle and Wade. Accordingly, some time about April 1796, the two latter invested the sum of £1,500 in the purchase of 3% Consols, the first step in founding the School.

Following the demise of Sir Charles the new owner of his Harrietsham estate was, by the terms of the Will of William Horsmonden Turner, William Baldwin* who, with his second wife, Frances, must have moved into occupation of 'Stede Hill', which for a time had been known as 'Harrietsham Place', in 1796. At this period the Rector of Harrietsham was the Rev. J. R. Hayward.

On the 22nd April 1796, Sir Charles Booth's executors and trustees, Ruddle and Wade, wrote from the Royal Exchange to William Baldwin:

Sir,
    We do ourselves the pleasure of acquainting you that agreeable to the Will of the late Sr Charles Booth we have this day invested Fifteen hundred Pounds in the purchase of £2,238. 6. 1. Consol^d 3 p^{r}c^t Bank Ann^y at 67 p^r c^t in the name of Frank Ruddle and George Wade the Revd James Robinson Hayward† and William Baldwin Esqr. Also a farther Sum of Five Hundred Pounds in the purchase of £757. 11. 6. Reduc^d 3 p^{r}c^t Bank Ann^y at £66 p^r c^t into the said names for the distinct purposes directed by the Testator—the Deeds of Trust will as soon as convenient be prepared by our Solicitor, and

* See my *Stede Hill, The Annals of a Kentish Home.*
† Rector from 1773.

the carrying into effect the purposes for which the above is intended
remains now to be considered by the Trustees and settled on the best
possible plan that can be devised—we forbore the investment of
the Two thousand Pounds directed for the like purpose to the Parish
of Maidstone not yet being satisfied whose name as Vicar of the
Parish can be placed with the other Trustees named.

Deare Sir

to   Your very & V Hble Servants
Ruddle & Wade

Wm Baldwin Esqr.

Five days later a second letter arrived to announce that
£3,007. 10. 4. had also been invested in Consols 3% at £66 0. 2.
in the names of Ruddle, Wade and Baldwin:

> 'until there shall be a Vicar of Maidstone competent to have his
> name placed in the trust.'*

Two years elapsed before the school came into being, then
the Boys' School was opened about Lady-day 1798 and that for
the girls the following Christmas. No written evidence as to where
in the Village these Schools were located has come to light.

To judge by the character of the typography employed, the
small advertisement broadsheet, reproduced here, 'The Rules and
Regulations for the Schools at Harrietsham', must have been
issued about this time. As a reflection of the conditions of the age,
so vastly different from those prevailing today, the 'Rules' are
a remarkable commentary. Whether the relaxation of some of
these has benefited modern youth is a matter of doubt; the
reader must form his own conclusions.

Two references in the advertisement puzzled me—'the
Education of Children ... on the *Madras System*' and the third
rule which spoke of 'Master, Mistress and *Monitors*'.

As so often in the past when I have needed help and advice
over some notty point I applied to my old friend the Reverend
Doctor Brade-Birks, the erudite Vicar of Godmersham, who
quickly came up with the explanation, advising me to look up
the life story of the Scottish divine and educationalist Andrew
Bell. This I did. Bell was born at St. Andrews on the 27th of
March 1753. He graduated at the University there and, as a young

* James Reeve was appointed Vicar in 1800.

A KENTISH PATCHWORK

RULES

AND

REGULATIONS

FOR THE

SCHOOLS

Established under the Will of SIR CHARLES BOOTH, Knight,

AT HARRIETSHAM,

For the Education of Children in the Principles of the Established Church,
upon the Madras System.

1. CHILDREN to be admitted from five years of age and upwards.

2. No Child to be admitted unless free from every infectious disorder.

3. THE Parents or Friends shall engage for the punctuality, obedience, and cleanliness of the Children admitted; for their strict attention to the commands of their Master, Mistress and Monitors, and for their proper behaviour during Divine Service.

HOURS OF ATTENDANCE AT SCHOOL:—

4. EVERY week day (except Saturdays) from Lady-day to Michaelmas, in the mornings from 8 to 12, and in the afternoon from 2 to 5 o'clock; and from Michaelmas to Lady-day, in the mornings from 9 to 12, and in the afternoon from 2 to 4.

5. ON Sundays every Child to be at the Schools in the morning precisely at 10, and in the afternoon at 2, in order to proceed to Church, unless they reside at too great a distance, in that case, the Parents must cause them to attend at the Church nearest.

6. EACH Child on the Monday Morning to bring one penny in advance, towards the expences of their education and distribution as rewards to the deserving of both sexes, and for their Writing, Cyphering Books, &c. &c.

7. No Child to be absent from Church or School, (except in case of sickness), when immediate notice must be given to the Master or Mistress; in neglect of this, or of any of the foregoing Rules, the Child will not be again received into the School, unless satisfactory explanation be given.

N.B.—Prices at which Plain Work is done by the Girls may be had of the Mistress.

TIMES OF ABSENCE ALLOWED:—

EVERY Saturday; one month at Hopping; a fortnight at Christmas; and two days at Easter and Whitsuntide. During which time, it is requested that the Parents, as is their duty, cause their Children to read to them whenever opportunity will permit.

J. V. HALL, Printer, King's Arms Office, Maidstone.

graduate went to Virginia, U.S.A., where for some years he acted as a tutor. On his return to this country he took Holy Orders and in 1787 sailed for India where after two years he became superintendent of the male orphan asylum at Madras. Here he found his work hampered by a scarcity of teachers so he introduced a system of monitors under which senior pupils acted as tutors to their juniors. The system worked well and following his return to London in 1797 he published a small pamphlet explaining this educational innovation of 'monitorial' tuition.

About this time a Quaker named Joseph Lancaster started a school in Southward and in its running adopted Bell's principles although he claimed the idea was his own. The experiment proved highly successful and many Nonconformist schools then coming into being followed the Lancaster example. This proved a shock to members of the Church of England and in retaliation to the dissenters' efforts similar institutions were set up embodying Church of England principles and Bell was made superintendent of the newly-formed 'National Society for Promoting the Education of the Poor in the Principles of the Established Church'.

As the Harrietsham schools were opened in 1798, they must have been the first, or at least among the first, in the County to operate under the Madras system, the other three of the Booth Foundation, Maidstone, Horsmonden and Marden no doubt followed suit. Also the Andrew Bell story would seem to confirm that the advertisement broadsheet was issued about the turn of the century.

In 1812 the Harrietsham living passed from the Reverend Hayward to George F. Nott, D.D. This distinguished cleric was a Fellow of All Souls College, Oxford, Prebendary of Winchester, and Preceptor of History to the Princess Charlotte of Wales, Rector of Woodchurch as well as of Harrietsham. He resided partly at Winchester and partly in Rome, never at Woodchurch and very little at Harrietsham, a fact which caused some local discontent. In consequence the burden of administering the Booth bequest, the School and the Bread Charity, fell squarely on the shoulders of William Baldwin, a duty which no doubt occasioned him not a little worry.

In May 1820 the Squire wrote to the absentee Rector, a long letter dealing with the future of the schools:

'As it is uncertain when I may have the pleasure of seeing you and wishing to obtain your acquiescence in what I have to submit respecting the Charity Schools here, I have thought it necessary to address you. The house wherein the Schoolmaster used to Reside and teach was what is termed the Parish Poor House, Sr Charles Booth not having by his Will made provision for a S(chool) Room, but as until lately the Poor placed in it were sent to Hollingbourne in union with other Parishes for a Term of Years, the which being expired and the Agreement not Renewed, the Poor house being wanted for its original purpose, I have for some time past permitted the School Master to reside and teach in a Farm House of mine—but the Farm being (about) to be occupied by a fresh Tenant who will require the whole House, another place must be provided for teaching the Boys at that time. The Room in which the Girls are taught is by much too confined. The Husband of the Mistress, a carpenter, has offered at his own Cost, to erect on a piece of ground of mine, which he occupies, a Building for the purpose of teaching both Boys & Girls, on Condition (on the event of his Removal) be permitted to take down the Building. By one little extra Expense or other the Charity remains at this time above £50 in arrears with me so that although I readily would give a piece of Ground, yet having no surplus of the Dividends in my hands to erect a Building, I submit whether it may not be best under the circumstances to accept the man's offer?'

Dr. Nott did not reply to this letter so, in September, the Squire wrote again to him on the subject but still without success. Then, in the following April, he made another effort to get some action by the dilatory cleric and suggested that:

'a small piece of pasture Land of about 50 Rods belonging to the Rectory, of little value, if it could be obtained, (would provide a site on which) an appropriate Building might at reasonable expense be erected and I requested if agreeable to U that U would (as a Trustee) be so kind as to endeavour to obtain it for the purpose. I regret to have occasion to Renew the Request but unless the Grant is obtained I do not at present conceive how it will be practicable for the Boys to be taught unless in the Church which will not be altogether suitable.'

By the end of the 18th century the administration of poor relief, and also of many local charities designed to help the impoverished or to provide schools for the poor, was in a sorry state through inefficient or bad management. Then, in 1818, Parliament appointed a commission of inquiry into educational charities and a year later a similar commission to examine all charities for the poor. These inquiries continued until 1835 when a select committee of the House of Commons recommended the establishment of a permanent board to review the whole position and compel trustees to render annual accounts to safeguard charity property. This step led to the passing of the first Charitable Trusts Act of 1853 and 'the Charity Commissioners of England and Wales' came into being as a body.

Shortly after it was established the Commission of Inquiry into schools must have taken evidence from William Baldwin for in 1821, when two of the trustees of the Harrietsham School were — Springet and — Edmeads, he wrote to the former on the subject of the possible purchase from All Souls College, Oxford, of a small piece of the rectory land on which to erect a school building, the proposition he had already put unsuccessfully to Dr. Nott. The letter concluded:

'Another matter appertaining hereto I wish also to mention. When the last Deed of Trust for the Schools was made, the Solicitor in London blended those of Maidstone & Harrietsham together, which the Commo^{rs} of the Charity Schools when they examined me at Maidstone objected to, and requested that separate Deeds might be made which I promised to have done. I have mentioned it to Mr. Reeve (? a Maidstone trustee) but omitted it to Mr. Edmeads & will therefore thank you to do it & acquaint me with the result.'

Some eighty years later—1903 in fact—the Rector of the period, the Rev. C. B. B. Marshall wrote to the Board of Education for some information concerning the Booth Foundation and in reply received a transcript from 'the Printed Reports of the Former Commissioners for Inquiring concerning Charities' (Volume I, page 115), which provides interesting information concerning the running of the schools. At the time of the Report there were in the school thirty-five boys and twenty-six girls:

... taught upon the Madras system, reading, writing and arithmetic, and the catechism. The girls learn needlework and knitting.

The master has a salary of £25. and receives ten shillings a year for each boy, to the number of twenty, on condition of his keeping up that number. For whatever number he may have beyond that, he receives only one pound. He engages to teach forty. He has also five shillings a year for each girl who comes from the girls school to learn to write; of these there are generally from eight to ten. He has also some small allowance for keeping the accounts, and providing firing and stationary, making his whole charge about £44. 13s. He is allowed to take private scholars.

William Baldwin died on the 9th October, 1839, in his eighty-fourth year, and was buried in the Stede chapel of the parish church. In consequence, William Wriothesley Turner Baldwin, his eldest son, became the owner of the Stede Hill house and estate.

Understandably in the months which followed the new squire was much occupied in dealing with the many legal formalities which arose from his father's death, an occupation to which the contents of his Letter-book bears witness. Among the numerous letter copies of this period there is only one reference to Booth School matters. This is dated 20th December, 1839 and was addressed to Mr. Peckham, presumably the schoolmaster at the time.

You will discontinue from the commencement of the last quarter to receive Pence Money from any of the Boys at the Charity School and return them what has been received since Michaelmas. I will thank you to show this Note to Mʳˢ Fermor and request her to observe the same order towards the Girls at her School.

From this it would seem that Mrs. Fermor was the mistress of the girls school and that the boys and girls were taught in different places. It is also interesting to learn that the children were obliged to contribute 'Pence Money' towards the cost of their education. Whilst the amount so collected must have been comparatively insignificant it does in some degree belie the title 'Charity School'.

Some four years after William Baldwin's death an important event in the school's history came about, his son, W. W. T. Baldwin, made a gift of half-an-acre of land as a site upon which a school building might be erected. The ground was a part of the field known as Little Brickhouse Field and Meadow later destined to be cut into by the construction of the South Eastern Railway line and highway now known as the A20.

The Harrietsham School, 1973

A School Group, 1928.   Photograph by S. A. Pope
Note the Kent Rag Stone Walling

William Baldwin as a young man, from a painting
in the possession of Lieut.-Col. Edward Baldwin
The name of the artist is unknown

For the record it may be valuable to quote the Trust Deed in full:
Dated 9th May 1844

Wm. W. T. Baldwin Esq.,	DEED of CONVEYANCE of
to	a Site for Schools in
The Rector, Church wardens,	Harrietsham, Kent.
etc.	(5 Vic. *c.* 38).

Enrolled in Her Matys High Court of Chancery the Sixth day of July in the year of our Lord 1844 (being first duly stamped) according to the tenor of the Statutes made for that purpose.

80 2s
(Signed)
D. Drew.

HARRIETSHAM (KENT) SCHOOL TRUST DEED
I   WILLIAM WRIOTHESLEY TURNER BALDWIN

of Stede Hill in the Parish of Harrietsham in the County of Kent under the authority of an Act passed in the fifth Year of the Reign of Her Majesty Queen Victoria entitled an Act to afford further facilities for the Conveyance and Endowment of sites for Schools DO hereby freely and voluntarily and without valuable consideration GRANT AND CONVEY unto the Rector Churchwardens and Overseers of the Poor of the said Parish of Harrietsham and their Successors ALL that piece or parcel of land containing by estimation half an acre more or less situate in the said Parish of Harrietsham now forming part of a field called Little Brickhouse Field now in the occupation of John Walker which said piece or parcel of land intended to be hereby conveyed is bounded on the south by and abuts for the length of One hundred and twenty eight feet or thereabouts on the Turnpike Road leading from the town of Maidstone to Ashford in the said County and is bounded on the east by and abuts for the length of One hundred and twenty two feet or thereabouts on the parish Road leading from the said Turnpike Road and the Village of Harrietsham to the Church and Stede Hill and is bounded on the north by and abuts for the length of One hundred and fifty four feet or thereabouts on a field called Great Brickhouse Field belonging to me the said William Wriothesley Turner Baldwin and now in the occupation of Edward Norrington and is bounded on the west by and abuts for the length of two hundred and one feet or thereabouts on that part of Little Brickhouse Field aforesaid not intended to be hereby conveyed and which said premises are delineated in the Map drawn in the margin thereof TOGETHER with all easements appurtenances and hereditaments corporeal or incorporeal thereto

69

belonging or connected therewith And all my estate right title and interest in or to the same premises TO HOLD the same unto and to the use of the said Rector Churchwardens and Overseers of the Poor and their successors for the purposes of the said Act And upon trust to permit the said premises and all buildings thereon erected or to be erected to be for ever hereafter appropriated and used as and for a School for the education of children and adults or children only of the labouring Manufacturing and other poorer classes in or near the Parish of Harrietsham aforesaid and for no other purpose whatsoever. AND WHEREAS Sir Charles Booth Knight deceased late of Harrietsham Place now called Stede Hill in the said parish by his Will dated the eighth day of June One thousand seven hundred and ninety two directed his Trustees and Executors therein named to lay out the sum of One thousand five hundred pounds in some of the public funds bearing interest at three per cent to be invested and continued in the names of the Rector of the Parish aforesaid for the time being and his Successors and of the person or persons who should be from time to time the Owner or Owners and Proprietor or Proprietors of the mansionhouse and estate then called Harrietsham Place as aforesaid and in the names of his said Trustees and Executors or the Trustees to be appointed in their stead as the trustees of the said fund from time to time for ever and directed that the dividents interest and annual produce of the said trust fund should be applied by the said trustees for the time being or the majority of them for the providing and paying a School Master and School Mistress for the teaching and instructing of such poor Boys and Girls Inhabitants of or near to the said Parish of Harrietsham to read and write as the said trustees should think fit and with such powers and in such manner as in the said will is expressed AND WHEREAS it is intended forthwith to erect suitable buildings for the Schools of the said Parish in the same premises hereby granted IT IS NOW HEREBY DECLARED that the said Schools shall at all times hereafter be under the general control and management of the Rector of the said Parish and of the said Owner or Owners of the said Mansion House and estate for the time being and of any other person or persons who shall for the time being be a Trustee or Trustees of the said fund under or according to the said Will and shall be at all times open to the inspection of the Inspector or Inspectors for the time being appointed or to be appointed inconformity with the Order in Council dated the tenth day of August one thousand eight hundred and forty IN WITNESS whereof I the said William Wriothesley Turner Baldwin have hereunto set my hand and seal the ninth day of May in the year of our Lord One thousand and eight hundred and forty four.

William W. T. Baldwin

Acknowledged by the said William Wriothesley Turner Baldwin the party to this Deed at Maidstone in the County of Kent this fourth day of July one thousand eight hundred and forty four before me

(Signed) Henry D Wilder

a Master extraordinary in Chancery

Signed sealed and delivered as and for his act and deed by the within named William Wriothesley Turner Baldwin in my presence

(Signed) Walter B. Biddell (Baronet)

13, Old Square, Lincolns Inn, London.

Little time was lost in utilising the ground and by the end of the year or early in 1845 the school building, still in use today, had been erected. Thereafter as a result of the Booth bequest many generations of Harrietsham youth have been educated therein.

There are no references to this important transaction in the Baldwin Letter-book and later only one concerning school matters before the last letter copied into the book in February 1846. This Booth Trust communication is undated, but follows immediately after another letter marked 22nd August., 1844 so presumably it was written on the same day. It reads;

Miss Smithson at Mr Smithson at Oaten Hill, Canterbury. Mr Riddle was sorry not to be at Harrietsham and to have seen you when you called at Stede Hill. We have rec^d an unacceptionable (*sic*) Character as to your moral & general Conduct and not less as regards y^r capability as a Schoolmistress. We therefore offer you the Situation as Schoolmistress of the Harrietsham Girl's School at a Salary of £30. We think you will find no difficulty in suiting yourself with Lodging— You would not be req^d until Mich^s (11th Oct. next) from w^h period y^r Salary would commence. Any further information you require you will at all times receive by address^g Mrs Baldwin, myself or the Revd Mr Riddell.

W.W.T.B.

Bagshaw's *History Gazetteer and Directory of the County of Kent*, published in 1847, which contains much valuable information concerning the history of Kent villages, after quoting the substance of Sir Charles Booth's will, provides the following information about the building of the Harrietsham school:

'A handsome school was erected in 1844, at a cost of £420, of which £380 was raised by subscription, and the remainder paid by the Rev. Mr. Riddle, and Mr. Baldwin, the latter gentleman having given half-an-acre of land for the site. Mr. Martin (no doubt Wykeham Martin of Leeds Castle) also gave liberty for the stone to be got on his property.'

This latter statement would explain why the walling is built in Kent rag rather than the brickwork more customary at the period.

It may be appropriate here to recount briefly what steps were taken at Marden, Horsmonden and Maidstone to provide schooling to meet the expressed wishes of Sir Charles Booth. Marden it would seem was quicker off the mark in building its school than Harrietsham. According to Bagshaw 'In 1820, there remained the sum of £242 19s. unliquidated of the debt contracted in building and establishing the School, but as no means could be devised for discharging the debt out of the annual income, the sum of £1,492 10s. 9d. Consols, derived from Sir Charles Booth's gift, was sold out for the sum of £1,104 8s. 7d. Of this sum, £204 6s. 9d. was applied in part payment of the debt, and the £900 remaining was left in the Maidstone Bank, with a view of placing it out as soon as an opportunity offered itself. The money remained on this footing till December, 1825, with the Maidstone Bank, and £340 only has been recovered as the dividend. Under these circumstances the Charity Commissioners conceived that the trustees are liable to make good the loss, and as such thought it their duty to certify the case to the Attorney General'.

How this difficulty was resolved Bagshaw does not recount, but by 1896 a Public Elementary School had been erected at a cost of £500 for 180 boys, 134 girls, and 102 infants.

At Horsmonden, however, the story was a little happier, ten years passed after the Harrietsham school was built before a suitable building was erected there and then only with the financial help of the parson and his brother. Kelly's *Directory of Kent, 1907,* provides the details:

Practising Country Dances in the 1920s
Photographs by S. A. Pope

Cricket on the Booth Field

Brisk business at a Church Fete

'Horsmonden Endowed School (mixed) erected in 1853 at the cost of the late Rev. Sir William M. Smith-Marriot, bart. and his brother, the late Sir John Smith, bart. for 140 children . . . the endowment, amounting to £48 yearly, was left in 1707 by Sir Charles Booth.'

The Reverend Smith-Marriot was patron, incumbent and lord of the manor of Horsmonden. He was responsible for erecting the Victorian folly, no longer in existence, known as Scott's Tower.*

In Maidstone the Booth Charity still survives—periodically I receive invitations to attend meetings of the trustees—but the original school building has long since disappeared from the municipal scene. The Booth bequest amounting to £2,000 to provide 'a schoolmaster or schoolmistress, or both, to teach poor boys and girls 'inhabitants in or near unto the parish to read and write' was, wrote J. M. Russell in his *History of Maidstone*, 'accordingly invested and a school was opened', but where is not stated. Bagshaw (1845) provides the information. 'Trinity Church Model Schools, Wyatt-street, where 208 boys, 140 girls and 164 infants are instructed under the direction of the Incumbent of Trinity Church. Booth's Charity School, for girls, is incorporated in this.' While Kelly's *Directory* completes the story with 'Sir Charles Booth's school is abolished and the funds are now expended in continuation classes for scholars attending the National Schools in the town.'

From these random records it will be seen that the Harrietsham School building is the only one of Booth foundation to survive as originally planned, an important example of the mid-Victorian period when so many similar ones in Kent villages came into being and today are fast disappearing.

In May 1899, there was an important development in the Trust's history, Captain John Henry Baldwin, the son of W. W. T. Baldwin added to his father's gift by conveying 1 R. 22 P. of adjoining land as the site for a schoolmaster's residence. The Booth Trustees were able to arrange with the Charity Commission to use money of the Trust to erect a house—it cost £550 (and one penny!) but this sum had to be replaced out of the Charity income within twenty-five years.

* See *A Second Kentish Patchwork*, p. 84

The earliest Minute Book which has been found records a trustees meeting held at the school on 5th August 1903 with the rector, the Rev. Marsham in the chair. At this meeting the minutes of a previous one were read and confirmed so there must have been an earlier book. What a pity this has been lost—some-one must have been careless, could it have been one of the parsons?

The 1900 book was supplied by the Kent Education Com-mittee and bears the title on its binding, 'School Manager's Minute Book'. It was in use until 1st January 1964, when 'Per-mission was given to obtain a new Minute Book as the existing one had been filled'—all the 265 pages. This record of sixty-four years of administration by the changing trustees and managers, rectors of the parish, owners of 'Stede Hill' and others who served, although at times somewhat pedestrian in content, being con-cerned with the appointment or departure of members of the school staff, repairs to the buildings and such matters, is not with-out value and at times deals with matters of special importance. One such was the report made at the meeting on 8th October 1920, when it was learned from the Charity Commission that £971, Booth Trust money, in part used when erecting the Schoolmaster's house, had all been replaced. As a result the meeting discussed the possibility of using this accumulation of funds for the purchase of a suitable playing field or school recreation ground.

Opposite the school, immediately north of the railway embankment, was a field known as 'Woodreeves' and it was agreed to approach the owner, Mr. Fremlin, on the subject of acquiring this for the purpose. As a result, he agreed to let the ground at a rent of £12 per annum.

Five years later Mr. Fremlin died and his solicitors gave notice to terminate the tenancy. The school managers then opened negotiations for the purchase of the field and after some haggling a figure of £325 was agreed to. As the Booth Trust funds in hand were insufficient to meet this amount, Mrs. Buckingham, then lady of the manor and a trustee, offered to lend one hundred pounds (which was subsequently repaid) to enable the purchase to be completed. So early in 1926 the field became the property of the Booth Trustees to meet the recrea-tional needs of the school and the youth of the district and has been so used ever since, providing as it does a first-class cricket ground for the local club, tennis courts, and for the very junior members of the society a suitably equipped play-corner.

In August 1949 the Harrietsham School became 'Controlled', in other words it was merged as a unit of the Kent County Authority with a new Board of Managers. Thereafter, the Booth Trustees ceased to be concerned with the school finance and day-to-day administration.

Scattered through the pages of the Minute Book already referred to are references to a number of happenings and events in which the children played a part, treats, social occasions, awards and prizes given, and so on. One or two such entries concern the First World War period. For example, at a meeting on 23rd May 1917, there was 'Discussion of the question of providing dinners for the school children at a small charge, and it was agreed that it would save bread and be beneficial to the children if it could be arranged for'. This wartime measure was obviously the forerunner of the movement for providing school meals which now has been adopted throughout the country.

It was in the same year, in November, that the School managers were informed 'In response to the request from the Ministry of Munitions that horse-chestnuts should be harvested, the school children have collected about ¾ of a ton which have been fetched by Miss Baillie Hamilton of Greenway Court acting for the Ministry.' It would be interesting to know to what use the nuts were put; according to one authority (*The Encyclopedia Britannica*), I learn that from them starch, gum, mucilage, a non-drying oil, phosphoric acid, salts of calcium, *saponin*, by boiling which with dilute hydrochloric or sulphuric acid *aesculic acid* could be obtained. Also horse-chestnuts are valuable as feeding-stuff for grazing stock—sheep and cows. Given to the latter in moderate quantity they are said to enhance both the yield and flavour of milk.

A former pupil at the school during the headmastership of Mr. Matthews, Mrs Sylvia Willard, sent me a few of her memories of the period. On one occasion the late Duke of Windsor, then Prince of Wales, when travelling along the main road, stopped at the School and was presented with a bouquet by the youngest pupil, Joan Gray.

In June each year a fete was held in the Rectory* garden when the children gave displays of Country and Maypole dancing while at Christmas time a 'treat' took place in the School's main classroom and all present were regaled with slabs of cake and mugs of tea. On the last day of the Christmas term each child received a new sixpence piece given by Mrs. Buckingham in memory of her husband who lost his life early in the 1914–18 conflict.

"I also remember with sadness now," Mrs. Willard wrote, "although at the time we thought it exciting, how we all kept the two minutes silence (on Armistice Day) and our headmaster wiping away tears as he lost his only son in the Great War."

During the nineteen-twenties Stede Court was the home of the Ascherson family, the estate having been purchased by Mr. C. A. Ascherson in 1921 and from then on as owner of the house he regularly attended meetings of the Booth Trustees up to the end of 1930 when he sold the property to Sir Robert Gooch. Mrs. Ascherson and her two teenage daughters took an active interest in village affairs, the girls particularly in amateur theatricals (Renée, the younger, subsequently going on to win renown as an actress on stage and television) and in the Girl Guides' movement. Because of this latter interest in March 1928 Mrs. Ascherson purchased from a local farmer, one John Scott, who lived at nearby 'Ramchild', for Twenty-five Pounds, a small piece of land adjoining the Village Hall, with the object of erecting thereon a timber building for use as a Guides' hall and meeting-place. As recorded on the foundation which is still in position:

This Stone Was Laid
by
Lady Cornwallis
President of the Maidstone Division
Girl Guides
February 19th 1930

When the Aschersons left Harrietsham a Mrs. Mitchell, Guide Commissioner for the district, took over control of the local troop and jointly with Mrs. Ascherson and several other prominent residents acquired by purchase the site of the hall. Matters

* Now the Remand Home.

William Wriothesley Turner Baldwin about 1839.
From the painting by Sir William Ross, R.A.

Mrs. Dorothy L. Ascherson
when living at Stede Hill

Harrietsham School Fête held on the Booth Field, 14th July, 1971

remained thus until October 1950, when it was reported to the Booth Trustees that Mrs. Mitchell had offered to sell the property to the trust. Negotiations followed and as a result of these the Minister of Education made an order that the purchase for the sum of £175 of the property might take place by (to quote the official phraseology) 'The Educational Foundation of Sir Charles Booth'. So the 'Guide Hut' became 'The Booth Hall', a valuable amenity not only for the youth of Harrietsham but also for those not so young.

For a good many years the Glebe land lying north of the Booth Field had been earmarked by the Kent Education Committee as the site for new buildings to replace the original school, but the scheme failed to materialize. Then, on 5th January 1973, *The Kent Messenger* reported 'A new primary school is to be built in Harrietsham ... Work on the school is expected to start in the mid-1970s at a very rough estimate of £62,000', so it would seem that the original 1844 building with various additions made from time to time will for an indefinite period be called upon to serve the youth of the parish. However, when the new accommodation on the Glebe Field site does become available the ultimate fate of this early school building will remain to be settled. The hope of the Booth Trustees at the period will surely be that this not unworthy example of Victorian architectural taste shall be preserved and used to perpetuate the object of the Booth Trust in the furtherance of education in its broadest sense.

7

SAMPHIRE

ECENTLY when browsing through a curious work that I acquired a good many years ago as a result of looking through an antiquarian dealer's catalogue I became interested in the subject of Samphire. When the two small leather-backed books reached me I thought their contents, like their author, 'Pedestrian'. Published in 1801 the title page read:

FARTHER EXCURSIONS
OF THE
OBSERVANT PEDESTRIAN,
EXEMPLIFIED
IN A
TOUR TO MARGATE
IN FOUR VOLUMES.
By the Author of the "Observant Pedestrian," in two volumes,
"Mystic Cottager," "Montrose," &c.

On closer examination I discovered that the work provided many interesting sidelights on the life and times of the people of East Kent which changed my first impression. One short sketch among the many which attracted my notice was headed 'The Samphire Girl'.

Samphire, the word brought back vague recollections of Shakespeare's *King Lear* and the play's reference to the mighty Dover cliffe which now bears the bard's name. Promptly I looked this up, Edgar speaks:

> Come on, sir; here's the place—
>   How fearful,
> And dizzy 'tis to cast one's eyes so low!
> The crows and coughs, that wing the midway
> Show scarce so gross as beetles: half way down
> Hangs one that gathers samphire; dreadful trade!
> Methinks, he seems no bigger than his head.

In writing about the 'Natural History of Dover and the Scarce Plants found in the area' Edward Hasted in his History of the County listed *Crithmum marinum*, rock samphire and added the following footnote:

This is gathered here, mid-way down the cliffs, from a great height above; those, who follow this dreadful trade, being let down from the top, by ropes, in a basket for the purpose. This samphire, being a very fine flavoured sort, great quantity of it is pickled, and afterwards barrelled and sent up to *London*, and other places, as a great luxury for the tables of the opulent.

It is significant that Hasted should describe the Shakespeare Cliff variety of the plant as 'a very fine flavoured sort' an indication that less desirable varieties might be gathered along the Kent coast, in fact, I learned from my dictionary that *golden samphire– Inula crithmoides*, glasswort or *Marsh samphire* and saltwort, *prickly samphire* were commonly to be found along the British foreshores growing in rock crevices and were all used for the same purpose as the *rock* variety which would seem to have derived its name from the French *herbe de Saint Pierre*.

It might be expected that Mrs. Beeton would have been interested in the pickle which could be made from the long succulent glaucous leaves with their marked aromatic taste of this perennial plant, but in the early copy of her famous 'cook-book' which I consulted I could find no receipt for making the pickle.

The name 'glasswort' was used alternatively for *marsh samphire* because great quantities of the plant were gathered and burned to produce the soda used in the manufacture of soap and glass.

Writing about Shakespeare Cliff in 1847* Samuel Bagshaw described how the plant was gathered there in his day:

The rock Samphire is found on the cliffs here plentifully, the gathering of which employs some of the poor people, and is probably exercised now in the same manner as in the days of Shakespeare, by descending upon a stick fastened to a rope, which is secured above by an iron crow, or a stake driven into the ground at the top of the cliff; and when arrived at that part of the rock on which the Samphire grows, it is collected into a basket. The party then

* *History, Gazetteer, and Directory of the County of Kent.*

ascends by means of a rope, or is drawn up by his companions, upon a signal being given for that purpose.

The Observant Pedestrian's encounter with the Margate *Samphire Girl* would seem to make a suitable sequel to the above remarks on the plant's habitat along the Dover cliffs so below I quote this in its entirety.

Who this 'Observant Pedestrian' may have been is not disclosed but he claimed the authorship of several similar works and as the 'Tour to Margate' bears at the foot of the title page the information 'London. Printed for R. Dutton, No. 10, Birchin-Lane, Cornhill. By J. D. Dewick, Aldersgate-street', perhaps he was in fact R. Dutton and acted as his own publisher.

Pedestrianism in the latter part of the eighteenth and in the nineteenth centuries was a popular pastime for those with the necessary leisure and physical fitness. The names of some notable writers who were also well known as walkers which spring to mind include William Hazlitt, Thomas de Quincey, William and Dorothy Wordsworth, and Robert Louis Stevenson.

THE SAMPHIRE GIRL

I had passed two or three gay carriages taking their evening airings with company, across the solitary flats of the Isle of Thanet, and I was contemplating the well-known object of Hooper's Mill,* burnished by the glowing tints of a rich sun-set, when I came within sight of a young female, slightly clad in a tattered garb, but whose elegance of gait, and delicacy of form, particularly drew my attention. She was warbling a rural ballad, in tones peculiarly sweet, and on her arm she carried a large basket, apparently filled with herbage.

As I passed she dropped me a modest courtesy, which drew me instinctively, to glance at her features.

She was a very pretty brunette, with the most expressive eyes, fringed by the finest silken lashes I ever saw; and, as she modestly

---

* In 1801 Hooper's Mill must have appeared as very strange landmark, quite unlike the customary form of such buildings. Erected at the close of the eighteenth century it was the brain child of Captain Stephen Hooper, a horizontal windmill based on Persian prototypes. At the summit of a tall slatted tower was an enormous wheel provided with vanes like those of a ship's paddle-wheel that revolved in a horizontal plane to drive a shaft down the centre of the tower to the five pairs of grinding stones. This mill was working until after 1825 when it suffered severe damage in a gale and had to be demolished. There are various references to Captain Hooper's invention in *The English Windmill*. Rex Wailes. Routledge and Kegan Paul. 1954.

St. Lawrence High Street—from an early photograph

The Thanet Shore
Westgate to Margate

Shakespeare Cliff

Margate about 1831
The arrival of the Steamships 'Magnet',
'Royal Sovereign' and 'Dart'

Lighthouse, &c. Margate Harbour.

cast them downwards, and ceased her song, her rustic charms were heightened by a roseate blush that suffused her cheek.

'What have you in your basket?' asked I.

'Samphire, your honour; 'tis gathered from the rocks for pickling, and I am conveying it to the hotel at Margate.'

'And where do you live?' continued I.

'At St. Lawrence, your honour; my father is a fisherman, and my mother is a spinner.'

'And what are you?' said I.

'Any thing, almost, your honour, that I can turn my hand to, to earn a penny; but at Margate they call me the Samphire Girl.'

'And your name, fair villager?'

'Susan Woodley.'

'Aye, I like Susans mightily,' replied I; 'and if you are as good as one I've got at home, you need not be better.'

The girl smiled, but she made no reply.

'What do you expect for your samphire?' asked I.

'Four and sixpence, your honour, and that's a good help to a poor family, considering it cost nothing but my trouble. Times are so desprate hard, we must make money wherever we can; for it all goes, now-a-days, in bread, and little enough of that, too, God known.'

'True,' said I. 'Our staff of life seems reducing to a twig.'

'It does, indeed, your honour,' answered she, with a deep sigh; 'but,' continuing she, laying her hand on her heart, 'doesn't your honour think its owing to the cruel war?'

'I wish I could properly answer your question, Susan,' replied I, 'but that belongs to superior powers and judgement than mine to determine; in short 'tis a subject as dangerous as unpleasant, and so let's drop it.'

'The war,' resumed Susan, still harping on the theme; 'the war certainly affects some people, more than others, because, where you have no friend gone to battle, why you hear of it all without feeling it, like; because why, you don't see it in the first place, and in the next, it can't snatch away a father, a brother, or a—*any body* you esteem.'

The hesitating, *any body you esteem*, instantly touched the little vibrating chord of suspicion in my breast; I turned my penetrating

81

7

look on Susan, whose tearful eye dropped on the samphire she was arranging in visible embarrassment.

'Perhaps you have a brother there,' cried I, 'you speak so feelingly.'

'No,' answered Susan, 'only a friend.'

'A dear one, I fancy,' rejoined I; 'a sweetheart, fair Susan; and a true one, I hope, for your sake.'

The girl started, as if she had conceived me to be a magician, who had explored her inmost thoughts.

'Well, to be sure,' cried she, 'Ned Wilmott is a worthy young man as ever lived; he was our neighbour's son, please your honour—his father is a thatcher, an honest hard-working man—and his mother has never held up her head since poor Ned was listed. Oh, it was very cruel to *trap-pan* him away so, and tell him such a pack of fine tales about honour and glory. Ah! I shall never forget when he marched off through the village, in his red coat, after the odious drum; his poor mother said it sounded to her mind just like his funeral bell. He was a fine tall young fellow, just fit for a soldier, your honour, and the guinea they gave him, he left for me as a keep-sake; and what do you think he bid me save it for, your honour? I'm sure you can't guess.'

'Why, to buy a wedding gown, and a good dinner, most likely,' said I.

'La! your honour must be a *witch**,' replied Susan; 'for you have exactly guessed it; and so, your honour, I vowed a great oath, that I would never have no *lord* in the whole world but *himself*; and if I died before he came back, it should buy me a coffin.'

What an artless secret I had extracted. 'God grant him a glorious victory, and safe return,' said I, 'and with the blessing of success, you may both repose on a *bed* of *laurels*.'

Susan comprehended me not.

'Craving your honour's pardon,' cried she, 'I had rather have a comfortable *bed* of *feathers*; and if I ever live to see the happy day, I'll be married in a flowered chintz, with blue ribbons, and have a *leg of mutton* and *trimmings* for dinner; and if I knew your honour's name, I'd drink your health in a brimming noggin of ale, because you're such a good-hearted *kind* of a *gentleman*.'*

'Then, Susan,' said I, 'toast me as a queer-looking traveller, and his faithful dog, Trudge.'

* See comments in Postscript.

'Thank your honour,' replied she; 'I shall never forget that name; and when I take up our little brown can, I shall say, with all my heart, here's health and happiness to good *Mr. Trudge*.'

'Aye, aye,' said I, 'a man's never too old to be christened by a good name; and as I'm a trudger by will and nature, it's not an inapplicable one.'

By this time we had entered Margate, and the samphire girl, humbly courtesying her modest adieu, quickened her pace to the hotel, wither I entered also, just as she turned back from the door with her empty basket.

On a later occasion this Observant Pedestrian again encountered the Samphire Girl who had gone to 'the tranquil village of St. Lawrence' to deliver her ware 'at a sea-faring gentleman's house' from which he found her being led away in great distress by a kindly old woman.

As a child, it appeared, she had been warned against '*the black man*'—*the devil*, so 'when the servant opened the door, and grinned his black face, and stared with his great white eyes at her, down dropped she, basket and all, screaming out, Spare me, spare me; and so the more the man tried to life her up, the more she screamed, and at last *swooned* away; and so, when she came to, then they found out what was the matter, for she never *seed* a black man before in all her born days.'

'Mr. Trudge' did his best to pacify this young unhappy acquaintance by giving her a homily on ignoring the colour of men's skins—'Is the diamond less valuable because it is shielded in a *black case*?' he argued, and was pleased that by his words he was able to uproot 'such a prejudicial weed from an uncultivated soil.'

But all this is another story, one perhaps not without present-day application.

POSTSCRIPT

Shortly after the above was written a letter, headed 'Early Pedestrians' written by a Mr. C. J. Wright, appeared in *Country Life*. This referred to an article on Pedestrianism at the end of the eighteenth century by Brian Dunning.*

In his letter Mr. Wright was seeking information concerning other pedestrians of the period and this prompted me to inform

---

* Pioneers of Pedestrianism. *Country Life*, 5 July, 1973.

him about 'the Observant Pedestrian' and the 'Tour to Margate'. In making acknowledgement of this, Mr. Wright observed 'It is most intriguing. I wonder who the anonymous authoress was? It's not the sort of subject one would expect a lady to write on. She is considerably more racy that Mary Russell Mitford. Quite a puzzle in fact'.

His reference to 'authoress' did in fact puzzle me, for in reading the work I felt the average person would naturally assume the writer to have been a man, although there are some passages which might suggest it was a member of the fair sex, for example, the write-up of 'Seaside Adieus' with its close observation of feminine attire. If the anonymous author was a much travelling lady she must have been a formidable character; her somewhat sneering reference in one passage to 'the lords of creation' suggests that in a later age she would have joined the suffragette movement! Having formed this impression I wrote again to Mr. Wright and in reply he said: 'I see from your first letter that you speak of the 1801 edition of *Farther Excursions of the Observant Pedestrian* as being in two volumes. It seems, however, there must have been two editions that year, for the Bodleian copy is in four volumes. It is possible, then, that your copy lacks the preface, of which I enclose a reproduction, in which the author claims to be a lady. All the same I tend to your view and that, apparently, of the contemporary reviewers, that the style is too masculine to be a woman's.

My copy of the book, as the title page already quoted makes clear, is in Four Volumes, although bound up as two, and in fact, lacks the Preface pages included in the Bodleian copy. From the photostat sent me by Mr. Wright, I am able to quote the following:

TO THE

REVIEWERS IN GENERAL

Having already introduced to the world my Observant Pedestrian, whose brows have been crowned with laurel, without the incitement of a name, or patron to establish his celebrity; I have once more endeavoured to merit an equal portion of literary honour, by having complied with the solicitations of a numerous and respectable connection, in again collecting, from *truth* and *Nature*, the various annexed pages which compose the second tour of my Pedestrian:

and though I have not the temerity to shield myself with the aegis of Minerva, yet, conscious I am offering no prejudicial subject to inflame the credulity of youth, or offend the perspicuity of age, I rely on the clemency of that verdict the umpires of literary fate may please to decide, in proportion to its merits, or defects; but how will they be surprised to learn, that the subject is the sole effusions of a *female* pen, although the deep penetration of a *certain* critical class, could neither discern or imagine such ideas were composed by *woman*; and, in consequence of that opinion, rewarded, with liberal encomium, a production they could only deem credible, from the superior abilities attached to the liberal and more expansive system of education and worldly knowledge inherited by the *lords* of the creation. The Authoress, therefore, presents herself before your tribunal in her real feminine character, averring, she aims not the arrow of sarcasm at any peculiar individual; neither has she written with any lancet dipped in gall. Nature, as she is, has guided her humble quill, unbiassed by partial prejudice; she, therefore, with respectful deference, submits her embryo to the fostering breezes of the mild invigorating sunbeam of Hope, whose influence, she trusts, will disperse every chilling blight that may assail its feeble and unprotected bloom; with which encouraging idea, she has the honour to subscribe herself, the Reviewers most obliged and obedient,

Humble servant,

————.

Who then was this incognito wanderer in search of adventure and amusement? Study of the style of writing might perhaps provide a clue and research the answer.

Samphire

8

TWO KENT AUTHORS

MONG THE MANY WRITERS who have lived and worked in Kent are two who had particularly close association with the County, William Somerset Maugham and Robert Smythe Hichens. The former, the younger by ten years, spent an unhappy childhood and adolescence at Whitstable, the latter was born at the West Kent village of Speldhurst in 1864. Both had ties with Whitstable and Canterbury and as writers were achieving success at the turn of the century and in the decades which followed. Maugham's work is as valued today as it was in his lifetime, that of Hichens has largely gone into eclipse.

In my childhood at Whitstable the name of Maugham meant nothing to me; Hichens I came to know well although our friendship was of brief duration, shortly before and during the opening months of the 1914–18 war.

William Somerset, the youngest son of Robert Ormond Maugham, was born on 25th January 1874. His father practised in Paris as a solicitor in partnership with a Mr. Sewell at 54 Faubourg St Honorè. I learned the firm's address by a curious chance. My maternal grandfather, James Robert Pike, was a partner in a long established firm of solicitors with offices at Austen Friars in the City of London, and when working on the Maugham story, among a mass of old papers, I came upon an envelope which had never been posted addressed in my grandfather's copperplate handwriting (how beautifully solicitors wrote in those days) to:

> Messrs. Sewell & Maugham, *Solicitors*,
> 54 Faubourg St. Honorè,
> Paris.

86

It would be interesting to learn the nature of the business being transacted between the two firms, but now this is never likely to be known.*

Robert Ormond Maugham died in Paris in 1884 two years after his wife Edith, following the birth of her sixth son who lived only one day. The young boy, William Somerset, was thus left an orphan. Thirty-five years later he was to record the pathetic story of his mother's passing in his largely autobiographical novel *Of Human Bondage*. The nearest relative able to undertake his guardianship was the Reverend Henry Macdonald Maugham, incumbent of the parish of All Saints, Whitstable,† who had married a German-born lady, Barbara Sophia von Scheidlin. So it came about that the young Maugham was destined to spend the formative years of adolescence in the Victorian vicarage which was their home. With memories of his happy early years in Paris, speaking French almost as his mother tongue, inevitably he developed a hatred for the dreary building in Whitstable's Canterbury Road which ecclesiastical authority, lacking wisdom, had seen fit to erect nearly two miles from the parish church. 'It was a fairly large house of yellow brick, with a red roof, built about five-and-twenty years before in an ecclesiastical style. The front door was like a church porch, and the drawing-room windows were Gothic ... An imposing staircase led out of the hall. It was of polished pine, with a peculiar smell, and had been put in because fortunately, when the church was reseated, enough wood remained over. The balusters were decorated with emblems of the Four Evangelists.'‡

Maugham's memory of the town of his childhood, the Blackstable of the three novels, *Mrs. Craddock*, *Of Human Bondage* and *Cakes and Ale*, was much as I first knew the place.

'Blackstable was a fishing village. It consisted of a high street in which were the shops, the bank, the doctor's house, and the houses of two or three coalship owners; round the little harbour were shabby streets in which lived fishermen and poor people; but since they went to chapel they were of no account.'

* The full story of Robert Ormond and Edith Maugham in Paris is told in *Somerset and all the Maughams*. Robin Maugham; Longmans–Heinemann, 1966.
† Appointed Vicar, 1871, and succeeded in 1898 by the Rev. A. T. Theodosius.
‡ *Of Human Bondage*.

Just as Dickens mirrored his early life in *David Copperfield*, so Maugham drew on his teenage memories in these three novels. But those with knowledge of the district at the turn of the century cannot but be aware of the smallness of circles in which the Maughams moved, restricted to the main street and the western end of the town. Nowhere in the novels is there any reference to the one important house in the area, Tankerton Tower, or to the end of squirearchal rule over the Tankerton domain which came in 1890 when the land passed to a building-estate company. Did Maugham, in his schoolboy wanderings, ever explore the unspoiled acres of country bordering on the eastern cliff-top towards Herne Bay, or walk along the lonely beach between Whitstable Harbour and Swalecliffe? To this the novels provide no answer.

It is true in *Cakes and Ale** he refers to bicycling excursions with the Driffields. 'Driffield said that as soon as we felt sure of ourselves we must go for rides all over the county', but how far Driffield, Rosie and the narrator penetrated the more distant countryside is left unrecorded.

Often during his school holidays the lonely boy must have left the Vicarage and walked along Joy Lane to the beach at Seasalter. Thereafter, companionless, following the unfrequented shore towards Shell Beach and the isolated 'Sportsman Inn' on the edge of the marshes, on the way passing the solitary coastguard station with its long-obsolete battery.

Youthful memories of the solitude he found surely must have been drawn upon when writing the penultimate chapter of *Mrs. Craddock*.† 'Bertha's solitary walk was to the sea. The shore between Blackstable and the mouth of the Thames was very wild. At distant intervals, were the long low buildings of the coastguard stations, and the prim gravel walk, the neat railings came as a surprise, but they made the surrounding desolation more forlorn. One could walk for miles without meeting a soul, and the country spread out from the sea low and flat and marshy. The beach was strewn with countless shells and they crumbled underfoot, and here and there were great banks of seaweed and bits of wood and rope, the jetsum of a thousand tides. In one spot, a few yards out

* First published 1930.
† First published 1902.

at sea, high and dry at low water, were the remains of an old hulk, whose wooden ribs stood out weirdly like the skeleton of some huge sea-beast. And then all around was the grey sea, with never a ship nor even a fishing-smack in sight. In winter it was as if a spirit of loneliness, like a mystic shroud, had descended on the shore and the distant waters.'

And later 'Bertha loved the calm of winter, when the sea-mist and the mist of heaven are one, when the sea is silent and heavy, and the solitary gull flies screeching over the grey waters, screeching mournfully. She loved the calm of summer, when the sky is cloudless and infinite. Then she spent long hours, lying at the water's edge, delighted with the solitude and the peace of her heart. The sea, placid as a lake, unmoved by the slightest ripple, was a looking-glass reflecting the glory of the heaven, and it turned to fire when the sun sank in the west; it was a sea of molten copper, shining, so that the eyes were dazzled. A troup of seagulls slept on the water; there were hundreds of them, motionless, silent; one arose now and then, and flew for a moment with heavy wing, and sank down, and all was still'.

Here at Seasalter was the prospect recorded by Turner's brush eighty years earlier, which as engraved by Horsburgh, was entitled 'Whitstable', the well-remembered foreshore to which we walked from Tankerton to gather plants of the sea-poppy, the ubiquitous *glaucium flavum* which grew among the shells, for our 'Chiltern' garden. What a fantastic change the motor age has brought to this once desolate but fascinating stretch of foreshore—beach chalets, vast caravan parks, pleasure boats of many kinds, the attendant holiday crowds, with all the noise and litter they bring, have desecrated the beauty formerly to be found here.

The few miles of highway leading to Canterbury must have been thoroughly familiar to the lonely boy for in *Mrs. Craddock* Maugham based his description of Bertha's home on the still-existant house, 'Court Lees', set back from the road at the foot of Clapham Hill, only changing the name 'Lees' to 'Leys'.

'The house stood out in its squareness without relation to its environment. Built in the reign of George II, it seemed to have acquired no hold upon the land that bore it; with its plain front and many windows, the Doric portico exactly in the middle, it looked as if it were merely placed upon the ground as a house of cards is built upon the floor, with no foundations. The passing years had given it no beauty, and it stood now, as for more than a century it had stood, a blot on the landscape, vulgar and new.'

When, in 1955, Maugham came to write a preface for a re-printed edition of *Mrs. Craddock*, time had mellowed his architectural taste. No longer was he prepared to call the house in which Bertha lived 'a blot on the landscape' while, after half a century, he seemed to regret that each time he mentioned the building he did so with a sneer.

In the concluding chapters of *Of Human Bondage* it is obvious that Maugham was drawing upon his own local experience when describing Philip's stay with the Athelny family in the hop-garden at Ferne. We may guess that as a youth he must often have accompanied the Reverend Maugham on pastoral visits to the Whitstable folk who every September in large numbers went hop-picking at Hernehill to enjoy a few days away from the seashore and earn some extra money. Maugham's picture of a Kentish hop-garden and the life of the pickers is convincing and could only have been written by someone with close personal knowledge of the scene. 'The work was not hard, it was done in common, in the open air, and for the children it was a long delightful picnic; ... They went out in carts with bedding, pots and pans, chairs and tables ... They were very exclusive and would have resented the intrusion of foreigners, as they called the people who came from London; they looked down upon them and feared them too; they were a rough lot, and the respectable country folk did not want to mix with them.'

That under the name of 'Ferne' he was referring to the Herne-hill area, where hops had been grown since the 17th century, rather than the more distant Herne behind Herne Bay there can be little doubt. The hop-gardens nearest to 'Blackstable' were on the higher ground beyond the Seasalter marshes, the district now traversed by the 'Thanet Way'. 'It was under a mile from the sea' that Philip and the Athelny children, on their way to before-breakfast bathes, needed to cross over the marshland to reach the beach where 'the water looked cold and grey and Philip shivered at the sight of it',—the same stretch of foreshore which Maugham had described earlier in *Mrs. Craddock*.

Chapters VI to XXI of *Of Human Bondage* provide a vividly

remembered picture of Whitstable life in the '80s. Many of the characters introduced are easily recognizable by that rapidly dwindling number of natives and others who remember the town at the turn of the century, only the names have been changed by substituting those of other well-known local people. For example, 'Mr. Ellis at the Limes' who shared *The Times* with the Vicar was in fact Tom Gann; Wynn Ellis was the owner of 'Tankerton Tower' which the Urban Council is now pleased to call 'the Castle'.

The character of Josiah Graves, the bank manager of the novel, was obviously modelled on Sibert Saunders, the manager of Hammond and Co's bank, later a branch of the Capital and Counties and now Lloyds Bank. I remember him well, a dignified pillar of the church. He remained a churchwarden of All Saints' until the end of his long life, and was always a staunch Conservative.*

The Mrs. Wilson whose new bonnet provided such a welcome subject for discussion between Mrs. Carey, Parson Maugham's wife and the bank manager's sister, was in real life Mrs. George Holden, the wife of one of the town's leading ship-owners 'the richest man in Blackstable . . . thought to have at least five hundred a year, and he had married his cook'.

For long after her husband's death Mrs. George Holden lived on in the pleasant stucco-fronted villa in Oxford Street with its beautifully kept garden, one of the best in the town, which extended for a considerable distance by the side of the railway embankment. In her later years this charming and little old lady proved herself a generous benefactress to the town. When the contents of the house were sold by auction after her death I purchased a painting which had hung in the dining-room, a reputed Cuyp, but obviously a copy, which I still enjoy looking upon.

In the 1900s the town had three doctors. The one with the best practice, mainly among the gentry, was Dr. Hayward. He lived with his wife and two daughters in another stuccoed house in Oxford Street, opposite the George Holdens, and drove around in his own carriage, the only resident in the place who had one.

* See *The History of All Saints' Church, Whitstable*, I. W. Greene, Elvy Bros., Whitstable.

Second in importance as far as practice was concerned was Doctor Etheridge, 'old Etheridge' who looked after the health of the local Coast Guards and many of the locals who 'went down to the sea in ships' particularly the oyster dredgers and barge skippers.

The third of the trio was Doctor Wheeler who had a house in the centre of the town next to the Assembly Rooms by the Horse-bridge. Mainly he administered to the man-in-the-street and among his patients he numbered many doubtful payers, but somehow he managed to scratch a living.

Maugham must have known the Hayward family well for when his play 'For Services Rendered' was first produced, a study was made of the drawing room of the Oxford Street house and this was faithfully reproduced as the stage set. But the doctor's son whom Willie Ashenden—the I of *Cakes and Ale*—met in the High Street (Chapter XXIV) was young Etheridge, who had joined his father in practice as soon as he became qualified.

Maugham's description of his fellow O.K.S. as 'shabbily dressed and unkept' was both cruel and uncalled for. Commenting on this meeting Richard Cordell in his *Somerset Maugham** wrote 'When *Cakes and Ale* appeared, the Whitstable doctor† (a kinsman of Lord Nelson) was not offended by the unflattering description, for he recalled with amusement that when he had returned home after meeting his old schoolmate he had announced to his family, "I just saw Willie Maugham on (*sic*) High Street. I wonder why anyone with all his money dressed so shabbily". It was obviously a case of "pot calling kettle black!".'

The Ashenden name for the *Cakes and Ale* 'I' must have derived from Maugham's memory of another schoolfellow, Leonard Ashenden, who was at the King's School from 1881 to 1890. His younger brother, Harold Campbell and I remained lifelong friends from school and articled pupil days until his death in 1968. Why did Maugham use the Ashenden name, not only in *Cakes and Ale* but also in a series of stories? Was it because of a special schoolboy friendship or possibly the reverse?

The Driffield story is of particular interest in its relation to Whitstable social history of the '90s. When *Cakes and Ale* appeared in 1930 the use of the Gann and Kemp names was greatly resented

* Heinemann, 1961.   † He held the appointment of Admiralty Surgeon.

locally. Before Rosie Gann married Edward Driffield she had carried on with a Whitstable coal merchant, George Kemp. Maugham as a boy must have known of the respected local firm of Gann and Brown, Coal Merchants; perhaps their carts delivered fuel at the Vicarage. I very well remember the senior partner, Harry Gann, as a prominent townsman, always immaculately turned out, debonnaire, a flower in the buttonhole of his jacket, gaily twirling his walking-stick as he briskly strutted down the High Street, a character. Was it on his image that George Kemp 'generally known as Lord George owing to his grand manner' was modelled?

Sidney Brown, the other half of the Gann and Brown team was also a local personality. Interested in politics, a staunch Conservative, I knew him well from my school days when often we travelled together on the Canterbury-Whitstable Railway, to the 1930s when I was chairman of the Whitstable branch of the Canterbury Conservative Association.

When I first read *Mrs. Craddock* I gained the impression that Maugham may have had Sidney Brown in mind when he created Edward Craddock, the thrusting farmer who became politically minded and wished to adopt the name Craddock Ley or Ley Craddock, much to Bertha's disapproval.

But to revert to the Driffield story, it is significant that a character whom the young Maugham must have known about was a Mr. C. M. Driffield. A paragraph which appeared in the local press on 7th March 1891, reported

'At a vestry meeting the vicar (the Rev. H. M. Maugham) in the chair—the retiring Inspectors under the Lighting Act—Anderson and Halloway were re-elected and Mr. F. Kemp was chosen in place of Mr. C. M. Driffield, who had become disqualified by reason of his non-attendance to his duties'.

Also at the Seasalter vestry meeting, for the same reason, 'Mr. Driffield was not eligible for re-election.'

About the time the Driffields 'shot the moon', owing money to many Whitstable tradespeople, as well as three months wages to their maid-of-all-work, the Whitstable Oyster Fishery Company suffered a severe financial loss through the defalcation of the secretary and treasurer who absconded with several thousand pounds of the Company's money, none of which was ever recovered. Maugham must have heard the story which, years later, gave him the idea for the Driffields' moonlight flit.

On a fateful afternoon in September 1885, the vicar of Whitstable, accompanied by his nephew and ward, Willie Maugham went by train to Canterbury and from the West Station drove in a fly to the Junior King's School, a building in Palace Street screened by a high red-brick wall, which 'gave it the look of a prison' the boy thought. Today the building is known as *Walpole House*.

When making references in the book to the masters at the school in the 1880's Maugham intentionally disguised the real persons by transposing or giving them fictitious names. 'Mr. Perkins' in real life was, of course, the Rev. Thomas Field; the 'Gordon' who called the unfortunate Philip 'a club-footed block-head' was a disguise for the member of Dr. Field's staff, the Rev. E. J. Campbell, whilst the Rev. L. G. H. Mason, always known familiarly as 'Tar' became R. Turner. Woodruff and Cape's *History of the King's School, Canterbury*, contains contemporary photographs of the Masters in the time of Dr. Blore and Dr. Field.

The reference to the 'Black Book' that 'sombre volume in which the names of boys were written with their misdeeds' did in fact exist and the Maugham entry has been identified with the initials E.J.C. the Rev. Campbell appended, as can be seen in this reproduction of the relative section.

In the drawing-room the pair were met by the then head-master, the Reverend George Blore. To the timid nine-years-old boy, plagued by a stammer which remained with him throughout his long life, the headmaster 'seemed gigantic. He was a man over six feet high, and broad, with enormous hands and a great red beard; he talked loudly in a jovial manner; but his aggressive cheerfulness struck terror in Philip's heart' to quote Maugham's description of the meeting in *Of Human Bondage*.

The story of the years—unhappy years—Willie, as he was always called by members of the family, spent at the school, will be familiar to all readers of the 'Blackstable' books, and is fully commented on in *Somerset and all the Maughams*, while amplifying details were included in the long obituary notice written by that outstanding King's headmaster, Canon Shirley, for the December 1965 issue of *The Cantuarian* in which he wrote 'The trouble about

Part of a page of
THE KING'S SCHOOL BLACK BOOK
Showing the Maugham name entered for inattention.

"The Black Book was a sombre volume in which the names of boys were written with their misdeeds, and when a name was down three times it meant a caning."

Chapter XVI *Of Human Bondage*
by W. Somerset Maugham.

95

Of Human Bondage was that it was factual—there was hardly a thin disguise; men and buildings, the author "photographed" them all ... The hero, Philip Carey, suffered the deformity of a club-foot, and the mocking of masters and boys made him only the more bitterly conscious that he was not as others. Philip Carey was Willie Maugham, who had a bad stammer which remained always with him, so that he could never make a speech—he who had so much to say—and down to old age he found it hard to forgive those whose mocking made a bad thing worse. You see it in *Of Human Bondage*—the master glaring at him in a ferocious mood, "Speak, you blockhead, speak! Blockhead! Blockhead!"

Not long after William Somerset entered the school the Reverend Blore was succeeded, as headmaster, by the Reverend Thomas Field, the Mr. Perkins in *Of Human Bondage* whom Philip Carey adored in contrast to the assistant master, the Reverend B. B. Gordon of the story. 'Tar' Mason, one-time King's Scholar, who as a clergyman, returned to teach at the School in 1871 remained until 1908.

I retain vivid memories of this formidable instructor who attempted to rule with a rod of iron and put the fear of Moses into small boys. When I was in the Lower School (later I escaped from Mason's clutches by entering the Army Class to specialize in Architecture and Drawing) he took us in Classics and Literature for the last period of the day, five to six o'clock during the winter and spring terms, and three to four o'clock in the summer term.

The winter and spring terms were particularly strenuous for young day-boys coming from a distance; breakfast at seven o'clock, train journey to Canterbury, followed by a walk via the Coal Yard in time to reach the School for Prayers at 8.30. After lunch games and prep till four o'clock followed by lessons till six o'clock. Another Whitstable day-boy, C. A. West,* who had to cycle to the Harbour Station from his home at Chestfield, and I were allowed to leave at 5.50 with just time to catch the 6 o'clock train home. Two other friends came daily from Ramsgate having cycled from Broadstairs. On wet days Tar would taunt George, the younger of the two, with the remark 'I suppose Emery you'll have to wear your mackintosh trousers' and the boarders would all laugh.

* The late Major General C. A. West, G.B. D.S.O., M.C.

Photograph by Douglas West

Whitstable Vicarage shortly before its demolition in 1973

All Saints' Church in the time of the Rev. Maugham

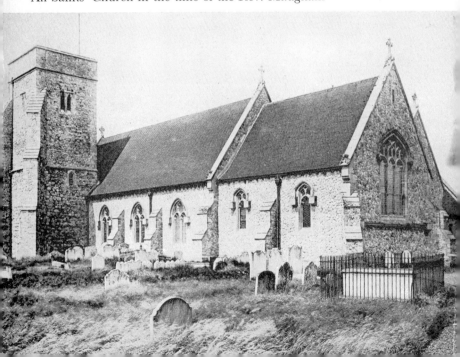

The Norman Staircase   The Dark Entry

The way to the King's School from Canterbury West Railway Station

Author's photographs taken about 1906

Whitstable, after the drawing by J. M. W. Turner

Seasalter, *The Battery, to-day* Photograph by Douglas West

I reached home at 6.30 p.m. except on Saturdays when it was an hour earlier, following the whole school's attendance at the afternoon service in the Cathedral. A welcome meal followed, then two hour's prep. By nine plus I was always ready for bed!

It was not surprising that at Tar's 5 o'clock lesson energy tended to flag and attention wander. Observing this his clenched fist would descend on his desk and he would roar 'Eyes in the boat there, Godsell'—he never got my name right!

Tar's classroom was in the Grange and on the first floor above were his sitting-room and bed-room. To reach these a long passage and the staircase had to be negotiated. Generally, once the class had settled down to work he would descend from his dais, thump along the passage and slowly ascend the stairs, either to answer a call of nature, or as many suspected, to enjoy a quiet nip of the 'creater'. However, before leaving, he would issue a stern warning 'If I hear a sound I'll string you all up to the gas-lamp and run you through with a rusty nail'.

Tar ruled by satire, which at times could be bitter, but my memories of him are not really unhappy ones, at times I found his quips amusing, he had a fine dramatic sense when reading English poetry. I still remember the effect when he recited 'How we brought the good news from Aix to Ghent'. Age, no doubt, had mellowed the Reverend Gordon since the time of Philip Carey. A vignette of another master etched into the portrait of the school is that of 'Winks'.

'Winks was the master of the upper third, a weak-kneed man with drooping eyelids. He was too tall for his strength. He gave an impression of lassitude. and his nickname was eminently appropriate.'

Maugham's description was a convincing one of the learned master of Classics, the Reverend L. H. Evans who joined the staff of King's in 1885 and so greatly helped many generations of the school's scholars. Although I was never in his class, to me he remains a well-remembered figure, for in appearance he was the living image of Sherlock Holmes as portrayed in the illustrations which accompanied Conan Doyle's stories of the great detective.

When recently the Whitstable Vicarage of the Reverend Maugham's time was demolished a school exercise book came to

97

light and was given to the King's School. There seems to be little
doubt that this was used by Maugham and one of the two duddles
on an end page is intended as a self-portrait.

, A CONCISE HISTORY OF, from the Com-
ement of the Christian Era to the present time.
ev. H. G. BONAVIA HUNT, B. Mus. 5th Edition.
ed. 3s. 6d.

OTHER MATHEMATICAL WORKS.

IMETIC. Comprising Logarithms, with
tions used by Artificers, Gaugers, and Lan
rs. By the late J. HIND, M.A. 9th Edition.

BRA, ELEMENTS OF. By J. HIND. 6th Edi
revised. 8vo. 10s. 6d.

OTETICS, OR THE SCIENCE OF QUANTITY. An
ientary Treatise on Algebra and its Groundwork
imetic. By ARCHIBALD SANDEMAN, M.A. 8vo. 20s

NOMETRY. The Shrewsbury Trigonometry
lementary Treatise. By J. C. P. ALDOUS, some-
Senior Mathematical Master, Shrewsbury School.

Part of a back page of a Greek school book found at the Whitstable
Vicarage, during demolition probably was used by Willie Maugham,
the lower doodle intended as a self portrait. Note the Eton collar.

One day in 1949 when I went to see Canon Shirley the subject
of Somerset Maugham's current interest in the school cropped up
and he told me how he succeeded in closing the breech which had
estranged the famous O.K.S. during the greater part of his life.
Shirley wrote to Maugham suggesting a reunion visit to the school
and asking him if he would become a governor. A year passed
without a reply.

'I thought to myself' said the Canon, 'This proves that the
fellow is really just the damned ---- (four-letter word) everyone
says he is. Then at last I received a very nice reply. My letter had
followed Maugham from one place to another all round the world'.

So the breach was mended and Maugham became a great
benefactor to the school. The Obituary written by Canon Shirley
recounts his many munificent gifts.

But was Maugham really reconciled after the damage his
unhappy school days had wrought, or was there some other reason

Robert Smythe Hichens,
about 1914

The Reverend Arthur
John Galpin, M.A.,
Headmaster of the King's
School, Canterbury,
1896–1910.
From a photograph about
1905

'Meadowside', Tankerton-on-Sea, Kent.
One time *pied-à-terre* of Robert Hichens

The author in his 6 h.p. Rover car in which he and Robert Hichens
made nightly journeys during August/September, 1914, when
inspecting Special Constables' posts

for his beneficence? In *Somerset and all the Maughams*, Robin Maugham suggested that there was. Another successful writer and O.K.S., but ten years younger than Maugham, was Hugh Walpole, who also made gifts to his old school. Was it in fact jealousy and the desire to out-do his rival that really influenced Maugham?

To me the particular fascination of the 'Blackstable' novels is the picture they provide of the Seasalter coast and hinterland as they were in the 1890s, we learn from them Maugham's reaction to the unspoiled natural beauty around him when he made lonely walks across the marshes or along the beach, storing impressions in his mind and recalling them so many years later when he came to write *Cakes and Ale*. It is sad to realize the changes this materialistic and noisy age has brought to this once lovely stretch of Kentish coast.

* * * * *

With justification—but only just—Kent may claim Robert Smythe Hichens as one of her more notable authors for he was born at Speldhurst on the Sussex border in 1864, his father, the Reverend F. H. Hichens being the parson of that parish.

When Robert Smythe was fifteen years old the Reverend Hichens decided to resign the living, give up all paid work—he was then a wealthy man—and move to Clifton in Gloucestershire.* Then, some five years later, the Reverend gentleman decided to return to the duties of a parish priest by becoming the Rector of St. Stephen's, Canterbury; about the same time he was made an Honorary Canon of the Cathedral.

In 1896 a bachelor parson, the Reverend Arthur John Galpin, was appointed Headmaster of the King's School in succession to the Reverend Field. Four years later, on 2nd January 1900, this young up-and-coming cleric, married in St. Stephen's Church, Miss Millicent Hichens, the Canon's youngest daughter, and sister of Robert. The couple were blessed with two children, christened Mary Cecilia and Michael John (the former always referred to by members of the School as Mary Kekilia, the hard

---

* The story is told at some length in the opening chapters of *Yesterday*. Robert Hichens. Published by Cassell, 1947.

'c' being favoured by the Greek pundits), who I remember from my years at the school, were often to be seen toddling about the Mint Yard in front of the Headmaster's House.

To provide a pleasant country-cum-seaside retreat the Reverend Galpin purchased a plot of ground in Tankerton Road, Whitstable, a few hundred yards from my parents' home and erected a small villa—barely more than a cottage—which appropriately was named 'Meadowside' for there was meadow land all around. Here the family spent most of their holidays and sometimes stayed briefly in term time also.

As the children grew older extra room was needed so the Headmaster decided to add a ground-floor room to provide a study. I watched the erection of this with considerable interest as I did all new building operations in the neighbourhood, for I was by now firmly determined to become an architect.

For some unexplained reason the new study was planned to project several feet in front of the rest of the house. This puzzled me for I knew there was a building-line laid down by the Tankerton Estate. So one afternoon when I encountered the Headmaster on the platform at Canterbury West Station I screwed up enough courage to ask him about it.

He was not in the least put out by my cheek and assured me everything was quite in order.

But was it? Two or three weeks later, when the structure had reached roof level, I noticed the 'brickies' hard at work pulling down the walls they had so recently erected. The Council surveyor had issued a notice of bye-law contravention and 'the cat was properly among the pigeons'. Someone, presumably the architect who should have known better, had blundered. I wondered how a fully qualified man came to make such a mistake.

Today the building stands much as I remember it in the first decade of the century except that now it is hemmed in on either side by houses of a later date—no longer does it live up to the name 'Meadowside'. In the recently taken photograph reproduced here I have attempted to show as nearly as possible how it appeared in the Hichens era. Even after these many years of exposure to the weather a vertical junction line in the brickwork can be noticed where the study, the single storey extension on the west side, was first raised, then pulled down and re-erected on the proper building-line. No doubt the architect had to foot the bill for re-erecting the building on the proper line.

In 1904 *The Garden of Allah* by Robert Hichens was published and its success was immediate; overnight the author became a best-selling novelist and by 1913 no less than 23 editions of the book had been printed. The Galpins lent him 'Meadowside' when they were not using it themselves and often, for short spells between visits to Sicily, Algeria or Egypt, he would take up residence at the cottage. Tankerton and Whitstable were thrilled to have such a famous writer in their midst. Frequently he could be seen walking or motoring through the town; sometimes his parents and his unmarried, eldest sister, Margaret, stayed with him at the cottage. His mother was an invalid and often he took turns to push her around in a bath-chair.

Hichens was a striking looking man, with his full share of good looks, always immaculately turned out, and at this period of his life, he was in his mid-40s, at the height of his success as a writer. He had first come to the notice of the literary world through the *Green Carnation* which had been published anonymously in 1894. This satirical comment on the aesthetic movement inspired by Oscar Wilde, as one authority put it, 'delighted hundreds of readers by the brilliant wit and charm of writing. In its finish and literary skill it was certainly a remarkable entry of a new author'. But Sir Compton Mackenzie in *My Life and Times*, *Octave Two* 'blows the gaff' concerning Hichens's quality as a witty writer—'Reggie Turner with his perpetually blinking eyes was the most consistently and effortlessly witty man I have known. R. S. Hichens had enjoyed the advantage of Turner's company up the Nile some years earlier and by making notes he had produced anonymously *The Green Carnation*, for Hichens himself was incapable of wit. That ghastly farcical novel of his called *The Londoners* condemns Hichens as a humourist.'*

I must confess when I got to know Hichens well in August 1914 I never found his conversation, although always highly entertaining, in the least witty.

Among the Hichens novels which appeared round the turn of the century *The Woman with the Fan* was the most successful, but it was not until *The Garden of Allah* was published that he achieved

* Quoted with Sir Compton's permission.

the rank of the 'best sellers'. From then onward his work output was prolific but none of the subsequent novels achieved the same success.

It is true *The Call of the Blood*, which appeared in 1906, was within two months of publication reprinted seven times, but no doubt much of the demand must have been stimulated by the success of *The Garden of Allah*.

Bella Donna (another best-seller) I suspect, may have been largely written at Tankerton. It made its début in 1909 and the dramatic theme obviously lent itself to stage presentation. The book was adapted as a play by J. B. Fagan and put on at St. James Theatre with Sir George Alexander and Mrs. Patrick Campbell in the leading roles. It was an instant success, the staging was first class, particularly the Egyptian scenes, and when I saw it in 1911 I was greatly impressed, it was such good 'theatre'.

When Hichens took up residence at 'Meadowside' he installed what the locals considered to be a more than adequate domestic staff, 'one man, four domestics' as one put it! There was a cook, a particularly snappy line in parlourmaids, an Italian gardener named Jacques, and the flamboyant Sicilian chauffeur, Carmelo Longo, who drove the novelist's imposing 'Austin' limousine. This colourful character with his dark hair, flashing eyes and magnificent mustachios not only caused many a heart flutter among the Whitstable damosels but after the outbreak of war in 1914 got himself hauled up before the local bench for exceeding the speed limit in Canterbury. In giving evidence a Police Constable estimated the car's speed at 30 miles an hour! Longo was fined 20s.

'My Sicilian chauffeur, who was in my service for a great many years', Hichens recalled in *Yesterday* 'was, like many Sicilians, a sometimes difficult but an always devoted servant. He, poor fellow, lost his health in the war of 1914–18, when he served in the Italian navy, and I had reluctantly to pension him off. He had, long before this, married and at the time of writing, still lives in his home in Sicily, an invalid looked after now by his daughter and her husband. His wife died many years ago. I often write to him and receive dictated letters from him in Italian.'

My first introduction to this literary 'lion' came in August 1913, when he wrote to me from 'Meadowside':

'My brother-in-law, Canon Galpin, has given me your name as an architect. I am thinking of adding a room to this cottage and should like to see you about it if possible.'

I duly met him, we discussed the subject, and I went away to prepare plans, but shortly after he wrote again. 'I am exceedingly sorry that circumstances have resolved me against building onto this house. I am advised that it would be a mistake to build onto a house that I only rent by the year. It's disappointing but can't be helped." (This letter is reproduced on the next page.)

This did not surprise me. From the first it seemed obvious that, had the project materialized, such an addition would represent a free gift to his brother-in-law. It was none of my business, but the incident was perhaps a pointer to a certain lack of business acumen in his make-up.

In 1913 my father died after a long illness and both my mother and I felt we needed to get away, preferably to somewhere on the Continent. Because of its wealth of great architecture— classical remains and medieval—I had for long wished to visit Sicily, and as my Mother had no particular preference as to where we should go, we set out for Italy and Sicily early in January 1914.

After a short stay in Palermo and a visit to Gergenti we arrived at Taormina where Robert Hichens had a villa not far from the Roman theatre. Having met him so recently I felt it would be nice to look him up. Unfortunately, although he had established himself in the town for the winter, he was, for a short time away in Egypt and so we did not meet again until the following August.

In *Yesterday* he penned a long description of this delectable Sicilian town where each year, until the 1914–18 War made the journey impossible, he spent the winter and spring months and recalled the many notable persons who figured among the British set.

When the spring came Hichens returned to Tankerton and was often to be seen out walking. One evening after dinner I plucked up courage and called on him, armed with a batch of black and white prints and colour transparencies which I had taken in Sicily. His reception was most kindly, we had a long chat about Taormina and after he had looked at my photographic efforts he produced some large and very fine prints, the work of a Taormina

Meadowside
Tuesday

dear Mr. Goodsall,

I am exceedingly sorry that circumstances have resolved me against building onto this house. I am advised that it would be a mistake to build onto a house that I only rent by the year. It is disappointing but can't be helped. Please will you let me know what I owe you. I am sorry to have troubled you for nothing. Yours sincerely

R. Hichens

. George Holden

t : Dr. Charles E. Etheridge

Photographs from the Douglas West Collection

Cross, Whitstable, about 1900

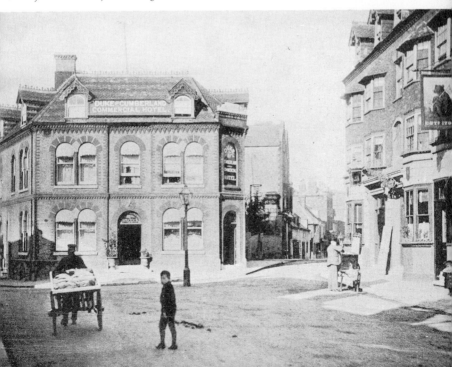

The author's wife having her fortune told by the sand-diviner in Comte Landon's garden, Biskra, on the 8th February, 1921. 'The Diviner dropped his fingers on the pyramid, lightly pressing the sand down and outward'—*The Garden of Allah, Book III*

Taorming below the snow-capped summit of Etna
From the author's photograph taken January 1914

photographer who specialized in the portraiture of Sicilian types, mostly boys and young women; many of the photos would have graced the walls of any important exhibition of photography.

While in residence at 'Meadowside' Hichens did not entertain to any great extent. His only regular guests, in addition to the Galpins and his mother and sister, were the Spenders—Alfred Spender was the famous editor of that fine newspaper, *The Westminster Gazette*.

'While I remained at Tankerton', Hichens wrote in *Yesterday*, 'my loneliness there was mitigated by the frequent presence of my friends, Mr. and Mrs. Alfred Spender, who came down nearly every week for two or three nights from London, as Mrs. Spender was running a hospital there for wounded and ill soldiers,* and, when he could spare the time from his work in London he helped her in the organization of it. They were both devoted workers, and I was glad to contribute something to aid in the finances† and often visited the patients.'

By chance when preparing this manuscript for the press among a package of old papers I came upon the first year's Report and Accounts of the London Hospital Convalescent Home at Tankerton, issued in 1900. The Committee members were: Mrs. Montague Crackanthorpe, Mrs. Alfred Harmsworth, Miss Lückes (Matron of the London Hospital), the Hon. Sydney Holland (Chairman of the London Hospital), Frank Lloyd, Esq., and Alfred Spender, Esq., the Hon. Secretary being Mrs. Alfred Spender.

At this time the London Hospital in the heart of the East End 'dealt with nearly 12,000 in-patients each year'. The Tankerton Convalescent Hospital 'was opened on June 24th, 1899, over 100 men have been received, and with only two exceptions—both hopeless cases from the first—successfully treated'.

As a youngster I had become bitten by the amateur theatrical bug, encouraged by two older school friends, Edward and Allen Roper, whose parents lived close to my parents' home 'Chiltern'. Together we put on shows in our own 'theatre'—actually a large purpose-built wooden hut which an indulgent grandfather had

---

* After August 1914.
† Appeals for support in the *Westminster Gazette* helped materially to finance this Convalescent Home.

erected for us in the 'Chiltern' garden. My special forte at that time was conjuring, ventriloquism, monologues and comic songs. Later this activity led to my taking part in or organizing local charity concerts. In January 1909 I was responsible for arranging a 'Grand Musical and Dramatic Entertainment' in the Whitstable Assembly Rooms in aid of the London Hospital Convalescent Home. Most of those taking part were professionals and after paying all expenses the sum of £11 14s. was handed over to the Home. Because of this effort, and a number of subsequent small shows put on at the Home itself, I got to know the Spenders before I met Hichens.

Occasionally there were visits of local friends to 'Meadowside', particularly H. B. Irving whose country home was the Black Mill at the top of Borstal Hill. 'Harry Irving was splendid company . . . and often came to dine with me. I knew also his wife, the charming Dorothea Baird, and his two very attractive children.* Another visiting friend was the Canterbury solicitor, Henry Fielding.'

'Meadowside' and the Parade above the Tankerton Cliffs was described by Hichens in *The Dweller on the Threshold* published in 1911.

'Minors' as he named 'Meadowside' in the novel, was "a delightful little red doll's house—standing in a garden surrounded by a wooden fence, with the downs undulating about it. Not far off, but behind it, was the sea. And the rector, pointing to a red building in the distance, on the left and much nearer to the beach, said:

"That is the hotel where the professor must be staying, if he is here"—the Tankerton Hotel where, in fact, the Spenders often stayed. Later "Mr. Harding asked Malling (two of the characters in the story) if he would like to take a stroll. They put on their coats, and went out, making their way to the broad, grassy walk raised above the shingle of the beach. The tide was far down, and the oozing flats were uncovered. So still, so waveless was the brown water that at this hour it was impossible to perceive where it met the brown land. In the distance, on the right shone the lights of Herne Bay, with its pier stretching far out into the shadows. Away to the left was the lonely island of Sheppey, a dull

---

* One of these, Laurence, has been my friend since these distant days. See my *The Eastern Rother*, pp. 84–85.

shadow beyond the harbour, where the oyster-boats lay at rest. There were very few people about: some fisher-lads solemnly or jocosely escorting their girls, who giggled faintly as they passed Mr. Harding and Malling; two or three shopkeepers from Whitstable taking the air; a boatman or two vaguely hovering, with blue eyes turned from habit to the offing."

This was a convincing picture of the Marine Parade as I first knew it, a mile-long walk that Hichens often made. It was a favourite 'constitutional' of mine also in those now far-away days.

Shortly after the Declaration of War in August 1914, the Kent police started to enrol Special Constables throughout the County and the great spy scare began to develop. As I had opened an office in the town and had a number of architectural commissions on hand, I felt I could not just walk out on these and join up as so many young men were doing. But service with the 'Specials' was a different matter and I volunteered for this duty as soon as the appeal was made. About the same time Hichens also enrolled. Many years later he recalled this in *Yesterday*.

The Whitstable 'Specials' had quite a big area to cover extending from the Ham Shades railway bridge at the eastern boundary of Tankerton to the 'Red Sluice' on the Seasalter marshes, with a look-out point on the high ground south of the town known as 'Fox's Cross', as well as several miles of the foreshore.

Nightly vigils were made at a number of points, roads, bridges and vantage spots, manned by two or three men at each with reliefs taking over at four hourly intervals. Someone had to make routine visits to these posts and carry back any reports to the headquarters established at the Whitstable Council Offices in Oxford Street. As I had a car and could drive I was picked for this duty whilst Robert Hichens, probably because he lived so conveniently near to me, was deputed to be my 'half section'. Thus it came about that each night, often at some unearthly hour like two in the morning, I would pick him up at 'Meadowside' and we would set off on our long drive round the district, a drive made difficult by having to use dimmed side-lights, which in those days were only oil lamps!

Later in the war Hichens was plagued by insomnia which he attributed to "the fact that during the many months of my sojourn in Tankerton at the beginning of the war I had often been obliged to be on duty at all hours of the night. Every twenty-four hours I had had four hours of police duty, and these hours had taken me all round the clock. Sometimes I had been out at night, watching by bridges or railway lines, from ten until two, from eleven until three, from twelve until four, and so on. My sleep had continually been interfered with".

After the lapse of over thirty years when he came to write *Yesterday* memory must have played him false. I never recall him 'watching bridges and railway lines'. I certainly never did; our nightly motor rides round the countryside left no time for such dreary vigils.

Hichens proved a most entertaining companion. He was a great raconteur, as his autobiography proves, and I enjoyed his company enormously. Of the many stories he told me several remain fresh in my memory. One concerned his friendship with the then ageing Maude Valérie White, the French-born pianist and author of many popular ballads of her day; she is often mentioned in the autobiography. One evening when the two were staying on Lake Como they had gone out together after dinner in a motor-boat on the lake, with a local boatman in charge. It was moonlight and the boat sped swiftly across the still water hemmed in by the black mass of encircling mountains, a perfect setting for happy conversation. Suddenly, Hichens told me, he saw that the boat was heading swiftly for some stone walling bordering the shore and horrified he realized that the boatman was fast asleep. He leapt for the tiller and in the nick of time steered the craft in a sweep away from the masonry. A moment later there would have been a head-on crash.

Some catacombs in Algeria were the scene of another adventure. Accompanied by his chauffeur, Carmelo Longo, who always travelled with him abroad, Hichens attempted to explore the maze of underground chambers. In the absence of a local guide they quickly became lost and after expending some considerable time trying to find the way out, with a rapidly failing electric torch as the only form of illumination, the situation began to look serious. Then, in the far distance, they saw a patch of daylight breaking through a fracture in the roof. This aperture proved to be just big enough for a man to squeeze through and by climbing onto Hichens shoulders his burly Sicilian companion was able to gain a handhold and draw himself up to the ground above. He went off to find help and after some while returned with two Arabs and a rope. It was then an easy matter to pull the adventurous novelist to safety. Subsequent examination showed that the escape hole was only a few hundred yards from the spot where they first entered the catacombs.

A characteristic American story concerned the stage production of *The Garden of Allah*. Hichens crossed the Atlantic to advise the producer and watch rehearsals. On the quayside, when the vessel arrived, he found himself ringed by reporters seeking his opinions on all manner of subjects including of course the forthcoming play. Perhaps unwisely he refused to be drawn and with difficulty managed to escape from the crowd of newsmen. Later, after he had reached his hotel, he was standing by one of the windows of his apartment which overlooked an internal court when he heard someone enter the room. He turned and remarked casually to the intruder. 'How do you do, how quiet it is here'. Then he realized the man must be a reporter and would say no more. Next day editions of the New York papers came out with banner headlines, 'Hichens says New York's quiet, what hell's he come from?'.

The spy mania, which arose immediately after the war was declared, obsessed everybody. Whitstable folk caught the complaint badly. German spies were landing nightly on the beach they asserted but no one could actually swear he had seen one, agents on shore were despatching messages by pigeon-post, so many flying birds were shot but not a single scrap of paper was found on any of them, above all, at night, unexplained winking lights were observed, flashing seawards. Surely these must be passing vital information to enemy submarines lurking in the Thames estuary the natives argued. It became one of the duties of the 'Specials' to investigate these reports.

One curious happening was never satisfactorily explained. From the road-junction at Fox's Cross, a narrow lane leads downhill past St. Alphege Old Church to join the then main road from Whitstable to Faversham; it was not until the twenties that the Thanet Way was cut across the Seasalter marshlands. At the junction there was another 'Specials' duty-post with a third at the Red Sluice where the highway runs close to the beach and since the East Coast floods of the 1950s has been protected by a massive sea-wall.

On our nightly journeys Hichens and I always travelled over this route. One night the men on duty at the two marshside posts reported seeing the undimmed lights of a car following us down the lane from Fox's Cross. Later inquiries showed that no car had passed the men at the top, moreover no car had emerged on to the main road below. All the way the lane was enclosed by hedges or fences and there were no gates or other gaps whereby a car could enter or leave. The same thing happened on several subsequent nights but although the 'Specials' at Fox's Cross kept an especially sharp lookout they observed nothing and no car ever passed the point.

The mystery was never explained and after a time the lights were seen no more. Perhaps they were a vagary of imagination on the part of the watchers below, or could it have been that a gremlin was up to his pranks?

The most ridiculous episode Hichens and I were called upon to investigate concerned my friends, the Ropers', former home 'Kingsbury'. When they moved away to Sussex shortly before the war, the family which followed them remained unknown to all the neighbours; they kept themselves strictly to themselves, in fact, I never learned their name. When the spy scare was at its height there were reports that lights in the house were kept burning far into the night which at the back could have been seen from the sea. The coast towns had been warned to keep all lights dimmed although no complete blackout was enforced.

Hearing of this report Hichens and I decided to keep watch, and one night, a little before twelve, we took up our position in the field opposite 'Kingsbury' (of course the ground is all built over now) and awaited developments. The dining-room lights shone brightly and behind the drawn blinds the silhouettes of figures passed continuously back and forth. For some three hours we continued to watch. All the time the lights shone in the room and the occupants moved about but it was quite impossible to guess what task they were engaged upon. However, their activities certainly looked sinister we thought.

As the night was distinctly cold and we were getting nowhere

I suggested a different line of investigation, I would use my hobby of photography as an excuse to gain entry into the house in daylight.

Next morning, armed with my camera, I knocked at the door, introduced myself to the housewife, and asked permission to photograph the adjoining 'Tankerton College' playground from one of her back bedrooms. Of course I knew the house intimately and felt my excuse would seem a valid one to explain my call. If any signalling had been going on it would have been from Allen Roper's former bedroom.

The permission was granted and I *pretended* to take a photograph—there was no good reason to expose a plate, they cost a penny each! Of course I found nothing and my detective effort seemed a complete waste of time. Nevertheless within a few weeks the house became empty—the mysterious birds had flown. I often wondered what they had been up to in the small hours, but of course I shall never know.

One evening Hichens, returned from Canterbury, was all agog with some exciting news which had been imparted to him by friends who lived in the Old Dover Road. These friends had a gardener who had a mate who, at Canterbury South station, had seen a trainload of Russian troops pass through on the way to Dover.

For the next few days the whole City buzzed with the story—the Russians had come, but strangely enough this was always recounted at second or third hand. Actually one could never run to earth the man who had seen the troops with his own eyes.

War nerves always breed wild rumours. Soon the whole of England believed the myth which authority never attempted to quash; perhaps it was merely a propaganda stunt. No explanation was ever forthcoming although it was suggested that someone had seen a contingent of men from the Scottish Highlands who, mistakenly, were taken for those of our eastern allies; alternatively, was a trainload of suitably disguised 'tommies' sent all round the country in an attempt to mislead the Germans?

In another Whitstable spy story neither Hichens nor I were involved. At the top of Borstal Hill there lived, in a mock-16th-century cottage, a retired colonel and his wife. This gallant soldier became so worked up over the local rumours of spies and secret agents in our midst that the possibility of the danger developed into an obsession. At mid-day one Saturday he could stand the strain no longer, so, betaking himself to the station, he caught a train for London. Upon arrival he went immediately to the War Office and demanded to be interviewed in the highest quarter. The commissioner on duty at the entrance, probably out of long experience, smelt a rat, and after some delay arranged that the voluble visitor should be seen by an unimportant junior officer.

Patiently this young man listened to the, by now, somewhat irate ex-Anglo-Indian 'fire-eater' and as the long story of the Whitstable spy-ring was unfolded he realized the unwelcome visitor must be got rid of as quickly and tactfully as possible. So in classic manner he passed the buck.

'This is not really a matter for the War Office, Sir' he interjected, 'It concerns the Nore Command'.

'Very well' roared Colonel ---- 'I shall go and see the Admiral immediately.'

Down below the Colonel demanded to use a telephone and proceeded to make two service calls. One was to Victoria Station which was informed that 'Colonel ----, speaking from the War Office' was on his way to Sheerness. If no train was scheduled to leave within half-an-hour a 'special' must be laid on. Then he rang the Nore Command to give warning of his advent there.

These messages, originating from the War Office, duly impressed the railway officials and the Senior Service. Upon arrival at Sheerness Colonel ---- was met by a naval officer detailed to conduct him to the Admiral. By this time the hour was getting late so he was invited to dine in the Mess before the interview. He must have told his story convincingly for the Nore Commander decided on immediate action. A warrant officer and a party of blue-jackets were ordered to go to Whitstable in a double decker London bus and investigate.

So, with his naval party of spy-catchers Colonel ---- returned to his home town in triumph and spent the rest of the night beating up the whole district. The record of what they found, if anything, must surely lie buried somewhere in Admiralty archives!

My spell as a Special Constable was not of long duration. I left the town to commence what proved to be my somewhat varied war service. Hichens departed also—to London, where he continued his Special Constable duties for three years, his beat lying in the west end—Bond Street, Jermyn Street, St. James's Street, and in front of the American Embassy in Grosvenor Square. I never met him again although one or two letters passed between us. He never returned to Tankerton.

After the war was over—in 1920 I think—Arthur Collins put on a lavish production of *The Garden of Allah* at Drury Lane, with all its trimmings, the sand storm, the camels and a host of Arab performers dressed in authentic costumes which Collins and Hichens had collected at Biskra. Domini was played by Madge Tetheridge and the Monk by Godfrey Tearle. There had been many forebodings that the show would prove a flop, but "from the first night the play was an enormous financial success and the prophecies of Arthur Collins were entirely falsified ... Collins told me afterwards that *The Garden of Allah* was one of the greatest money makers Drury Lane ever had in spite of its tragic ending".* My wife and I saw the production and greatly enjoyed it. From the book three separate films were made by American film producers.

Another post-war theatrical success was Hichen's *The Voice from the Minaret* put on at the Globe Theatre in London with Marie Lohr and Henry Ainley playing the leading roles. We enjoyed this also for it was a charming and colourful production.

Memories of my association with its prolific author were revived when my wife, my mother and I made a holiday trip to Algeria in 1921. Understandably Biskra was on our itinerary. Sometimes I turn out the batch of photographs I took then and am reminded of the fascination of this picturesque oasis and its teeming native life.

Naturally we visited Count Landon's famous garden and my wife had her fortune told by the sand diviner "The Diviner squatted down once more on his haunches, stretched out his fingers above the sand heap, looked at her (Domini) and smiled".† If he was the same man Hichens knew he must have been very old. More probably it was some other Arab who carried on the tradition which he found profitable. Anyway he looked the part

* *Yesterday.*
† *The Garden of Allah.*

and was accepted without question by the many tourists who came to see and consult him.

How many people today read the books of Robert Smythe Hichens? Few, I suspect, compared with the number who made him a best selling author in the early part of the century. He must adequately have represented the light-reading taste of his era, taste so very different to that of this brash and permissive age.

BIBLIOGRAPHY

In the course of writing this book the following sources of information have been consulted:

Archaeologia Cantiana	Volumes annually since 1858.
Bagshaw, Samuel	*History, Gazetteer and Directory of the County of Kent*
Hasted, Edward	*The History and Topographical Survey of the County of Kent*, 4 vols., 1778. Revised edition, 12 vols., 1797.
Bucknall, Rixon	*Boat Trains and Channel Packets*, 1957.
Daly, Augustus A.	*History of the Isle of Sheppey*, 1904.
Igglesden, Charles	*A Saunter through Kent with Pen and Pencil*. 30 vols., 1900–35.
Ireland, W. H.	*History of the County of Kent*, 4 vols., 1827–30.
Harris, John	*History of Kent*, 1719.
Jessup, Ronald	*Kent* (Little Guides), 1950.
Maidstone Civic Archives	*Records of Maidstone*, 1926
Mee, Arthur	*Kent* (The King's England), 1936.
Kelly's *Directory of Kent*	
Kent Newspapers	*Kentish Post and Canterbury News Letter* *Kentish Gazette* *Maidstone Journal*.

INDEX